before we jump the broom

JAY HURT

before we jump the broom

The Premarital Guidebook for African American Couples

Tandem Light Press

Tandem Light Press
950 Herrington Rd.
Suite C128
Lawrenceville, GA 30044

Tandem Light Press paperback edition 2021

ISBN: 978-1-7341261-8-1
Library of Congress Control Number: 2020947546

Biblical passages are from the New International Version

PRINTED IN THE UNITED STATES OF AMERICA

I would like to dedicate this book to my lovely wife, Tawanna.
I look forward to living our pre-marital counseling together for the world to see
for the next sixty years. I love you!

Contents

Acknowledgments

I'm incredibly blessed that I have been surrounded by people who believe in me, support my creative process, and encourage me to pursue the things I believe can help others. What I have learned through this process is that there are people who support you, people who sharpen you, people who take you to task and people who hold you accountable. Each and every one of those people helped inspire me to write this book and I can't thank you enough. I find myself in a community of people who believe in each other and work to help each other grow. I'm honored to have friends, family, teammates and confidants who help me grow consistently. I hope I'm able to give to help you as each of you have given of yourselves to pour into me.

First of all, all gratitude and honor to God, who is the unquestioned author of my life. Many of His words are quoted in this book, but Ephesians 5:21-33 stands out to me for context of this writing. Submit to one another, out of reverence for Christ. Husbands, love your wives as Christ loved the Church— and gave Himself up for her. This book is about how to set a standard for your family before marriage. God gave us a standard for marriage. He also gave us grace. Use both, His standard and His grace to strengthen our marriages. I thank Him for the blessing of His word.

Let me keep it 100, this book doesn't happen without the strength, courage, values, respect, loyalty and love of my awesome wife, Tawanna. I appreciate her patience as I wrote this book. I thank her for her feedback as I was writing. I also appreciate her for always being willing to work through the challenges that come with marriage. She's simply amazing. I love you, Babe!

Inspiration comes from a lot of places, but one of the places it really came from during the writing of this book is the plethora of awesome people in my life. I want to start through this list by honoring great men in my life. Their relationships with their wives and how they speak to other married couples encourages me. Our conversations are great, but I also see how they honor their wives and how they pour into the lives of others. I'm truly blessed to have these men and their families in my circle.

Lamar Tyler – Thank you for being a great friend. I appreciate the conversations we have about business and life. Watching you grind for the past several years to reach the level of success you have reached is truly inspiring and I'm wishing for more success and blessings for you and your family as you continue to grow and elevate the community. Thanks to your lovely wife and business partner, Ronnie Tyler, as well! Looking forward to hitting the golf course more often and watching your Eagles lose to my Cowboys! Thank you for being an inspiration.

Derek Q. Sanders – Iron sharpens iron. Most of the time when we talk, we are sharpening each other and encouraging each other. Our friendship is a great example that I hope others can appreciate. You and I don't agree on every topic all of the time, but we share our viewpoints, we respect the other person and we learn from each other. That's the way it should be. I appreciate your wisdom.

Paul C. Brunson – I watch you take calculated risks, win some, lose some, but yet move forward more determined to win the next time. You are truly an inspiration to me. I can't tell you how much I appreciate your words of support and your belief in me to work with you. Please allow me to also thank your awesome wife, Jill Brunson, as she keeps me in line with these projects we work on! Looking forward to continuing to empower people together.

Stephan Labossiere – You have been incredibly humble and supportive of me in every way. I really appreciate the talks at Atlantic Station, strategizing or just talking about life and how we navigate the journey. Watching you connect with your audience in an authentic way is something I strive for and I appreciate your insight and your friendship.

Lawrence Henderson – Leadership can be taught, but I believe there are traits of a leader that some have more naturally than others. I think you are an example of a natural leader. I appreciate your wisdom and our conversations about life and leadership. Looking forward to hanging out and working on more projects together.

I also have amazing women in my life. These women all bring something different to my world. One thing that is consistent, each of them bring a measure of love and support that is unfathomable. I'm so honored to have each of these women as friends, mentors, and people I can confide in.

Deana Jo Vivian – It's hard to quantify the amount of respect that I have for you. Each time we talk, I'm always impressed by how thoughtful you are of your profession, your peers and your church. You have a knack for being articulate and keeping it real, all at the same time. I genuinely appreciate you.

Dr. Pamela Larde – Where do I begin? Amazing is probably not a strong enough word when it comes to you. You have an incredibly kind heart and you want to see everyone win. We battle at times because of our strong personalities, but ultimately, we are always working to make each other better. You also constantly put me to work! I appreciate it, though. I appreciate the support of you and your team with this book and I'm incredibly appreciative of the Academy of Creative Coaching. Looking forward to taking over the world!

Shellie R. Warren -- If there is ever anyone who keeps me on my toes, it's you! If you and I are iron sharpening iron, I should be a machete by now. I appreciate your conviction. Even though we don't always agree, I respect your conviction about what you believe more than anyone I know. Keep speaking the words of life and truth over others.

Kristina, Jalen, Jaesha and Jaydon (daughters, niece and nephew) – All of you guys mean the world to me. I love you all with all of the love I have to give. I'm putting you together in this acknowledgement for this reason: All of you are young adults at this stage. Your adult life is beginning. Now is the time you will begin to figure out things on your own, without parental advice or control. My prayer and hope for each of you is that you foster relationships based on the best decisions for you. Not under pressure, duress or some feeling of lack or loneliness. If someone could have told me something at your age that would have influenced me the most, it would have been that every decision you make at 22 or 25 will influence your life at 42 or 45. I hope you make informed, wise decisions in your relationships. Your lives inspire me to be better.

Tandem Light Press staff – Caroline, Lee, and other TLP staff. I can't thank you enough for helping to create this work. I'm a writer, but nothing about this is really easy for me and I appreciate you making the process as easy as possible. I hope I didn't get on your nerves too much and if I did, it's all

Pamela's fault! Seriously, I really appreciate the entire TLP team and thank you all. Looking forward to the next one!

My clients – A lot of what I have learned comes from real world interactions in sessions, masterminds, etc. I have some of the best clients a relationship coach could want. They are real, they're candid, they are sensitive and heartfelt, and I think most of all, they want the truth. They want healthy relationships and marriages. They want to feel empowered and honest enough with themselves to make the right decisions going forward. You guys inspire me. I hope our sessions together and the information in this book help you to pull out what you already have inside of you and ultimately create the happiest marriage you could hope for.

Introduction

There was a time when couples didn't get pre-marital counseling. Marriage counseling in the US began in the 1930s. Back in the day, we got married on the premise that this was a good decision to begin our families and move them forward. We learned how to adjust to our circumstances and environment. We made marriage work.

The fact of the matter is, many of our parents, grandparents, and great-grandparents tolerated each other. It was deemed acceptable. Whatever the challenge, make the marriage last and work through it. Love was not thought to be the foundation of marriage, but a by-product.

The reality, especially in the black community, is that marriage was a cornerstone of the community, but there were a lot of broken people in these marriages. They wanted to love each other and honor each other, but they didn't have examples and they didn't know what real honor and commitment looked like. People essentially tolerated each other's brokenness, because they didn't have much choice.

In today's society, this doesn't have to be the case. As a relationship coach, I have talked to many singles and married couples. In some cases, the challenges aren't all that different than they were for our people in the 40s, 50s and 60s, the difference is we cover it up better. We live in nice houses, drive expensive cars and have six-figure careers. Often, we still struggle with the PTSD of slavery, the reconstruction, and aftermath of Jim Crow. We put a tailored suit or a nice dress on it. It's the same struggle, only now in the information age.

I believe we can change the narrative on our relationships. I believe we can change the narrative on our marriages. That's what this book is about. When we are considering marriage, stop and take a look at what we are about to do. We're about to join two lives, that come from two different backgrounds, with different sets of values, morals, parenting styles, financial mindsets, sexual perceptions, notions of gender roles, and spiritual beliefs. It's worth putting in the work in this class to gain knowledge about yourself and your spouse that you might not yet understand.

It's really astonishing how many people I coach that think they know EVERYTHING about their significant other. When we get into finding out what we really know about each other, it is inevitable that couples always know a lot less than they thought they knew. It's important to find this out before marriage. It's not with the concept to try to break up a relationship, actually it is the opposite, it's to expose each other to the nuances of their spouse. These are things you need to know on the front end. People need to go in with their eyes wide open. After marriage, things we don't know become nuisances. Nuisances are just that at first, but they are like Chinese Water Torture, they become unbearable. You have to know what you are getting into to decide if you can rock with this little issue or not. When we have the power of understanding, that gives us the power of choice. When we don't understand, we feel like we didn't have a choice, which often leads to making a tougher choice later down the road.

One of the most important things I hope you get from this class and guidebook is that ultimately, you are in this together. You're not in this relationship to have the upper hand or for someone to come to you or do for you at your beck and call. Husband and Wife...you are in this together. Bonnie and Clyde, Sonny and Cher (they got divorced, bad example), Denzel and Pauletta, Barack and Michelle, you are in this. Together. Forever. Period.

Everything in the book may not apply to your relationship. That said, be honest with yourself. Be real about your situation. If something negative pops up and you realize it, it's not a death sentence to your marriage, it is something to work on.

Solomon 2:15 reads "...catch the little foxes that ruin the vineyards..." That's what you will find mostly in these pages. You will become aware of the little foxes. You can run them away from your marriage if you dig in and do the work to get them away from your vine. If it's a deal breaker for either of you, that's a different story. Most of you will already know your deal breakers before you take this class. If you don't know them, they will become crystal clear in these pages. One thought I have on deal breakers: They are called "*deal-breakers*" for a reason. Remember this if you run into one.

Finally, for everyone that takes this class, I hope this book and these sessions made you think. I hope you thought about what your marriage will really look like vs your preconceived notion of marriage in general. I hope you put a lot of time and energy thinking about what you bring to the marriage and what you can do to keep yourself healthy and engaged in your marriage each and every day. I hope you thought about your spouse, how awesome they are, what made you choose them, how they make you feel, where you see yourselves years down the road and why they thought so much of you they chose to spend their life with you.

I wish you a lifetime of love, health, happiness, amazing sex, enough children to love--yet keep your sanity, financial stability and security, fulfillment and blissful communication.

Coach Jay

Chapter One

"Dude, you just don't get it!"
How do we begin to understand our spouses?

In the beginning, there was man and woman. That's where many of our similarities ended. We walk differently, talk differently, act differently and of course think differently! God developed us to be there for each other. This is a fact, but it's also part of the reason we are as different as we are. Husbands love their wives as only Christ can exemplify (Eph 5:25-28). What many of us miss when we read that scripture is Christ gave himself up for the church. He sacrificed more than we can imagine. Husbands, the call to marriage is to be willing to sacrifice more than you may imagine. Sacrificing old habits, old relationships, even family if the situation is required. She's now your responsibility, your treasure, and ultimately your prize! Everything about her becomes a priority. Her well-being, her happiness, her wants and needs—all of it, becomes your priority.

I chose to start the guidebook here because one of the places where men don't always work hard enough in marriage is understanding. During this process, we will work on how to develop an attitude of prioritizing her wants and needs and working to understand what she is trying to communicate to you. We have a chapter dedicated to communication as well in this program, but we need to have clarity on how important it is to prioritize and work on understanding your spouse.

Understanding isn't a one-way street. Wives have to be ready, willing, and able to try to understand their husbands. Listening is always a two-way street. The thing for our community is that we have to learn how to listen to each other. Marriage is not easy. Marriage is a daily—yes, a *daily*—commitment to learn each other better and grow together. The commitment is the foundation. Once you make an executive decision that you are in this for better or worse, through sickness and health, until death do us part, you have confirmed to God, the world and, most importantly, your spouse, that you are committed to learning how to understand them.

Now that we have established that we are 100% committed to understanding each other, how do we do that exactly? Let's explore some ideas, then let's ask some questions.

Your Perspective is Fine... As Long as You Agree with Me

One of the things that will help both spouses understand each other throughout their marriage is giving their spouse the space to have their own perspective. Whether your spouse is highly opinionated (like me) or fairly reserved, respect the fact they have a perspective. This will be difficult for most of us, because in most cases, this is a skill we aren't trained in very well. Try to see their side.

Here's a great tip: If you are discussing an issue, don't immediately respond, even if you have a thought. Wait at least fifteen seconds. In a conversation, fifteen seconds will seem like an eternity. Hang in there. Let what they said marinate on you for a bit. Try to absorb it, think about it. Try to mentally see how their perspective could work. If you give it time, your mind will start to be receptive to the other person's way of thinking. We don't do this exercise to necessarily change our minds. We perform this exercise to understand where they are coming from. Let's be clear, your spouse could have grown up next door to you or a thousand miles away. Either way, they grew up with a different set of beliefs and values. We have to understand each of us in the marriage sees the world differently, because we grew up with a different world view. The way we learn to accept each other's world view is to try to see the world through the lens of your spouse. Here are four obstacles to seeing your mate's perspective:

- Stubbornness
- Lack of Will to Try
- Incapable of Seeing More Than One Point of View
- Not Used to Opening Their Mind

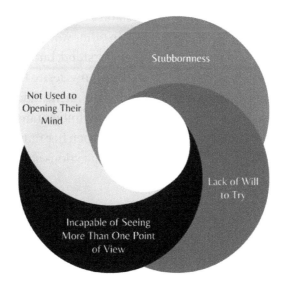

There are other challenges, but these four are the most common. We have to make a conscious decision to let go of stubbornness. *Stubbornness* is borne out of selfishness which we'll discuss. Stubbornness says, "I want things my way and I'm inflexible." Love says, "I sacrifice everything, including stubbornness when trying to understand my spouse."

Lacking a will to try is really more an expression of saying I want things my way. Again, a result of a selfish desire. Especially in the case of men, I don't know of a man on the earth who can't achieve what he wants to achieve when he puts his mind to it. This being the case, when we want to understand the perspective of our wives, we have to be willing to try at all costs.

Those who are *incapable of seeing more than one point of view* are people who were raised with a "My way or the highway mentality." If you are dating someone who is incapable of seeing your point of view, here's some news—they are never going to understand anything outside of their own viewpoint. I think it's crucial to understand we can't change people who don't want to change. If being understood is a deal-breaker and you are already swimming upstream in your relationship because your spouse is simply incapable of seeing your point of view, be clear that you have resolved your own situation: It's a deal-breaker. This deal can't close.

If your spouse *isn't used to opening their mind*, but willing, this is actually a step in the right direction. Anyone who wants to learn to understand the opposite sex can be taught how to do so. The fact that each man or woman communicates differently makes each person's level of understanding customizable specifically to their spouse. In other words, I can share something with my wife that she doesn't understand, but if she's willing to listen, I can break it down for her. I can make it my desire to help her understand, without getting frustrated or having an attitude. I want her to understand me, but if it's new to have to learn to understand someone else, then we need to work together on helping her open her mind. Understanding each other is a team sport. Let's look at some questions about understanding:

Conversation Starters

1. Are there times when you make a comment or ask a question and your mate responds, but their response totally missed the point of what you said? Share an example with your mate.

2. How often does your mate ask you how are you feeling? If often, what does your mate learn from your answer? If not very often, what could your mate learn from asking how you feel?

3. If your mate was to ask you if you are aware of the thing that bothers them the most about their work and the thing that bothers them the most about their home life, could you answer? Ask each other those questions, see how close your answer is and talk about their importance to your mate.

4. It's your mate's birthday! You can give them either a card, a nice piece of jewelry, spend the day with them, fix something broken for them or just give them a big hug and kiss! Which one would you do? What do they say is the right answer? When they confirm the right answer, talk about why their answer was right for them.

    _____

    _____

    _____

    _____

    _____

    _____

    _____

    _____

5. You seem to have a knack for knowing when to sit and simply rub her feet or give him a neck rub. How do you know when to do the thing that your mate needs the most? Talk about what that sense of understanding when to do the right thing at the right time feels like. What triggers help you know to do what your mate appreciates?

    _____

    _____

    _____

    _____

    _____

    _____

    _____

Why Understanding is Important

Many of us subconsciously believe great relationships run on autopilot. Therein lies the need for premarital counseling and premarital discussion. Autopilot is meant for planes and futuristic cars. The funny thing about autopilot is that even in the cockpit of an airplane, a plane has a predetermined flight plan with a set of parameters to follow. If something interrupts that plan, say a fierce electrical storm, the pilot is notified and the plan is altered and either taken over manually or put back into autopilot to continue the journey. The same is true of relationships.

The example of the plane having a course and then alerting a pilot for course correction is an example of understanding the relationship between a plan and the planner. Relationships are journeys. Journeys have a plan. There is course correction daily, but we take the time to create the plan, refine the plan, make sure that the people in the relationship understand the plan and then execute to the mission. Understanding is the point where we make sure everyone on the team communicates, agrees, and accepts how to move forward.

Much of what we are discussing on this guidebook is foundational to marriage, but make no mistake, working daily to understand each other is core to a successful marriage. Proverbs 3:13-14 reads, "Blessed are those who find wisdom, who gain understanding, for she is more profitable than silver and yields better returns than gold." The word "understanding" in this scripture is clarifying how important it is to understand what wisdom really entails. If one truly understands wisdom, he or she could profit in ways that are unimaginable. I want you to know if you can understand your mate, you can be blessed in ways you would never imagine.

Understanding each other comes with the knowledge that each of you see some things similarly and some things differently. It's paramount to know that every couple sees some things through the same lens and some things like they are from different continents. For example, there are some couples who might get together and one likes to eat crickets as a delicacy and the other thinks this is the nastiest idea ever! Neither is wrong, they are simply different perspectives. Learning your partner's perspective starts to give you a window into how they look at life.

EXERCISE

DATE: Feb 10, 2022

WHY UNDERSTANDING IS IMPORTANT

Let's take a moment to think about how we see life through our similarities and our differences. Take five minutes and each of you jot down three things you view as similarities and three things you view as differences.

GOD
CAREER GOALS
Dealing w/ Family

Finances
Talking in the moment
neither vs neither

After you finish writing them down, share the similarities with your partner and discuss how you find them similar. Do you agree on these?

Then after you have both shared similarities, share your differences. Do you find that you agree with your mate on these things being differences?

This exercise in perspectives will help you learn how your mate thinks. Most importantly, listen to why or why not they feel a certain perspective is similar or different. You will start to see into how they think. Listening is the key to understanding.

Finally, without impeding on the conflict resolution chapter, let's tie a bow around how perspective affects how we move forward through challenges and obstacles in our marriage. When we deal with understanding how to move through a challenge, one of the toughest things that everyone deals with is their own perspective. We want to jump to the conclusion because we believe we know how to resolve it. The fact of the matter is, both women and men would be served well by listening more. After listening clearly and confirming what you heard, then share your perspective and work together on the resolution.

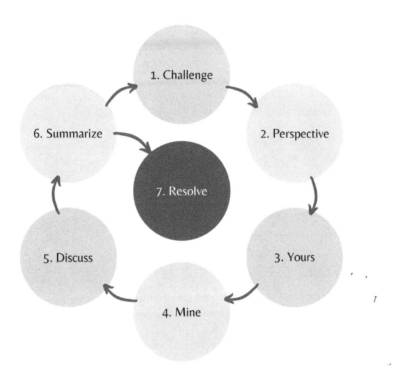

Flashback to this in your mind when you are overcoming challenges and you have opposing perspectives. Hearing what the other person is trying to communicate is more important than getting your point across and will go a long way toward resolving the situation.

Chapter Two

Self-Preservation is the First Law of Divorce

Dealing with inherent selfishness vs. developing selflessness as a character trait in our marriage

One of the most common preconceived notions about marriage is your new boo is here in this forever journey to *fulfill* you and *complete* you. When you listen to it on the surface level, it sounds romantic, even when Tom Cruise said it in Jerry Maguire. If you repeat this statement out loud to yourself, you will hear something else. Did you catch it? The statement is 100%, unequivocally about you! The statement is about what someone is doing for you or doing to you. Marriage, in its purest form, is not about you at all.

Marriage is not about someone completing you or fulfilling you. Marriage is about serving your spouse throughout the journey of life. Service will look different for every couple and every person, but essentially, service and sacrifice are foundational to the spirit of marriage. I mention the spirit of marriage because we get married for a lot of different reasons, but rarely will you hear someone say they want to marry because they want to sacrifice for their spouse. We're not wired like that. We are wired to take care of ourselves, at all costs, because frankly if we don't—who will? That's why marriage is incredible if we take the time to honor it the way it was meant to be honored. It's a contrast to our natural inclination as a single person. Our responsibility moves from ourselves to someone else.

Our nature tells us to preserve self at all cost. Self-preservation is our most natural instinct. To preserve, protect and defend...ME! Marriage really builds our character, because we have to learn to fight that instinct. That's why this chapter is dedicated to learning that our own wants and needs are superseded by the wants and needs of our spouse. The concept sounds simple, but it's hard to execute in practice because most of us are inherently selfish.

Selfishness is defined by Dictionary.com as: "devoted to or caring only for oneself; concerned primarily with one's own interests, benefits, welfare, etc., regardless of others." I have yet to meet a person who at some point wasn't selfish. The problem with selfishness in marriage is that married couples never fully recognize the greatness of the marriage if they don't put away their own selfish desires.

We want to get into the *how* of putting those desires away. We will discuss how to put away our selfishness, but first, let's use the following exercise to understand how we might be selfish.

Conversation Starters

Share three things you desire, right now. Let's make them things that are impactful in your life. We'll leave the cinnamon roll or banana pudding off for now. For example:

 Car
 New Job
 New wardrobe

MORE DINERO
NEW WARDROBE
HOUSE

Now take the most expensive thing you selected. I want you to take turns describing it to each other. Tell them things about it that other people may not be aware of—where it's from, how much it costs, where you can buy it, specifications about the item, etc. Tell your mate how you have planned to get it or how much you have thought about it.

Finally, I want you to ask yourself if you'd be willing to give up what you most desire. You've sacrificed for it; given your time, money, energy and resources for it. Would you, instead, buy the thing your spouse most desires knowing you would never get your desired item? This doesn't need to be shared aloud, but I want you to think about it.

As you think about your decision, how does it make you feel? Are you unsure? Does it immediately make you think of ways to compromise to get both things? Do you get a little indignant and say to yourself, *I love him/her, but I'm getting what I want*? Does it make your heart beat a little faster? Are you a bit insulted by even being asked to put what you want aside to pay for something for someone else?

_____

_____

_____

_____

_____

_____

Those feelings I'm describing above are the feelings associated with the idea that if we don't do for ourselves, no one else will. Selfishness has a negative connotation, but it's more than that—it's our way of making sure we are provided for, because we count on ourselves to ensure our provision.

The Bible is full of examples of where God himself or Christ made provision for others. Five thousand people came to hear Christ speak and they had no food. Jesus took a boy's lunch and made provision for the entire crowd. Marriage has the essence of this kind of provision. We have to be willing to take what we have to ensure our families are taken care of. This will probably look different for men and women and for people at different socioeconomic levels. The bottom line is, regardless of those things, we have to make a conscious, daily decision to put our spouse and their needs before our own. It's not a perfect science, but what being prayerful and repetitive in the decision to commit to your spouse's needs is key.

Selflessness is Not a Dirty Word

Do you remember growing up? There was always at least one child around who would give their lunch or their snacks to another child. There was always someone who would buy their lunch or be willing to split their lunch with another. There were people who, no matter how much or little they had, would make sure their friends were taken care of. There were another group of people who would try to take care of people even if they didn't know them. Those are the people who model selflessness for us.

In this era, it seems to me that sometimes when we see people give to others that they don't know, some of us believe they give with an ulterior motive. If we're being honest, it's easy to see how someone that could be popular could give to those less fortunate for the tax write-off and the brand recognition. Matthew 6:3 says when we give "do not let the left hand see what the right hand is doing." This refers to giving to the less fortunate and not to doing it in front of others for recognition.

Let's bring this mindset over to marriage. Husbands, when you honor your wives, speak well of them in public. Also, husbands, when you give and provide for your wives, do this in private. Selflessness is about giving to your mate of out of a pure heart with no recognition or expectation of return. It is important to understand, especially when giving doesn't come naturally to you, that you give because you love your mate and you want to do nice things for them, not out of a quid pro quo mindset (do for me and I'll do for you).

EXERCISE

DATE:

SELFLESSNESS IS NOT A DIRTY WORD

Write down three things that you have wanted to do but couldn't to this point in your life. It could be a trip to Africa, running a marathon, or running with the bulls (I'll help you build the courage to run with the bulls, but I'll be cheering you from the sidelines). It doesn't matter what it is, but let it be something you haven't been able to do for time, financial, or other reasons. Share these with your mate.

TRAVEL
GIVE MORE GIFTS
GO ON TOUR

Now, allow your mate to think for a minute and talk about how they can help you accomplish these goals. It may be a simple plan of attack. It could be knowing someone who can get you in the right streets with the right bulls (Is there such a thing as the right bulls? I digress...). They might be into fitness and have run marathons in the past. Maybe it's not of these things. The idea is that you each start thinking about how to proactively support your mate. There will be times to support in silence or just by being there. For the purposes of this exercise, I want you to proactively and intentionally support your mate.

EXERCISE

DATE:

LET'S PLAY A GAME

Let's play a game. This is best done in a group setting, but the exercise works for one couple as well. I want you to see how well you can support each other. Put a blindfold on your mate. Now, pick a prize for them (could be $25.00, could be movie tickets, etc.) Put the prize somewhere in the room. The next step is to guide your mate. You can guide them with instructions, but you can only give them five instructions. If you're in a group, the first couple to find the prize with only five instructions wins it. Now switch the blindfold to the spouse that hasn't worn it yet. Move the prize after the new person has the blindfold on. This exercise requires faith of one mate in the other. This also requires one mate to be the total support of the other mate. The more we believe in and support each other, the better our marriages become. We struggle with support as a community as much or more than anything in this guidebook. Black men have to be willing and capable to rely on and believe in the selflessness of the black woman. Black women have to require black men to be selfless and anything less is unacceptable.

Final Thought

Finally, for this chapter, take note of this concept: Selflessness is the key to unlocking the power and potential of your marriage. Everything in this guidebook will lead you down a path of strength in your marriage. Selflessness unlocks the real power. Have you ever heard someone say, "We'll be great together; we'll change the world." This is evident and likely true, but every couple who is great only realizes that greatness through the selflessness of their partner. I heard former President Barack Obama say First Lady Michelle Obama would have never chosen to be first lady or go through the rigors of senatorial or presidential campaigns without choosing to make a personal sacrifice. Mrs. Obama's sacrifice not only allowed her husband to be great in ways that history will write about, but it also showed her own amazing elegance and greatness to our country and the world. The selflessness displayed in this example is the same selflessness we all must have (be it husband or wife) to sacrifice for the greater good of the marriage. Selfishness is the first law of divorce. Selflessness is the first law of a true power couple!

Chapter Three

Listening with the Right Antenna

Learning to listen for clarification and understanding

I remember coming in my house one day and I asked my wife about her day. She was expressing frustration with something that happened at work. She was trying to tell me that there was a process in her role that was changing. She was explaining to me that this particular process was intricate to the entire system. Everything she does revolves around this process and it was changing. Having a background in corporate America, I immediately started thinking of ideas for how to incorporate everything with this new system. Put a visual to this conversation:

She's saying: *"Process is changing, but it's core to every function in our system."*

I'm hearing: *"Process is changing, system is staying the same. Let's figure out how to integrate the new process into the old system."*

This is how much of leadership at work, church, school, and other organizations listen. We listen to a story with the idea to complete it or fix it. However, when it comes to our partners, we have to work at simply listening. If I would have listened better, I would have heard that the company is already trying to do this integration. As her spouse, I wanted to help her fix a problem that didn't need fixing. But all she needed me to do was allow her to vent.

Active listening is comprehending, retaining, responding and paraphrasing the speaker's words for clarity. Listening actively is a good thing. Getting ahead of yourself because you didn't listen for clarity is not. Listening clearly is going to reduce the communication gap between a husband and wife significantly. Let's learn how to confirm you are clear on something.

EXERCISE

DATE:

LET'S SHARE

I want you to tell your spouse the two most significant things that you're enjoying about this book to this point. Have your spouse repeat it back to you, something like this (in your own words), "Okay, Babe, I like that the book is fun, and in every chapter the exercises are different." Repeat what you heard back to your mate. Don't write it down. Remember it. The instructor is going to ask a few people what their mate said. The mate can confirm if you were right or not. Ultimately, the point of the task is to see how well the mate can interpret what was said.

Keeping it 100

Can I be real with you for a moment and tell you why we struggle with listening? Real talk? The truth of the matter is we like to hear ourselves talk. Especially in today's culture where people are routinely struggling with being heard, we listen with the subconscious idea that we are waiting to get our next thought out. We aren't *really* listening, we're just waiting for our turn to say our piece.

Imagine if you were on a plane, the pilot suffered a medical emergency and you were the only person willing to try to land the plane. You put on the headset and you listen to Air Traffic Control. Push the stick forward. Lower the flaps. Lower the landing gear. Would you listen attentively or would you be trying to hear yourself talk? I guarantee you would be listening! You want to be like Captain Sullenberger who landed the plane on the Hudson River and walk away from this situation! You want to practice listening in this same manner when it comes to your spouse. Focus and receive the information from your spouse. Don't talk. Don't try to mentally anticipate what they are going to say. Simply listen. Confirm. That leads me to our next point: Marinate.

Trust the Process

Every person on the planet processes differently. Some people can answer a question almost before you can finish asking it. Some need time to think about things, even to the point where they may need to get back to you on it. Most of us can process some things faster than others. I have coached clients who respond quickly to everything, because sometimes their desire to be witty overrides their desire to be compassionate with their spouse. I have had clients who sometimes don't know how to respond, so they never respond. We don't want to follow either extreme. Let's begin to consider processing at your pace anything your spouse asks of you and everything they would like a comment or feedback on.

I call processing information from your spouse marinating. I want you to sit in your response for as long as you need to. You can respond in a millisecond or two days, but either way, let's learn to consider our spouses needs and feelings before we respond.

I believe as Christians, we are called to consider how others feel, rather than speaking our mind and letting the chips fall where they may. 1 Thessalonians 5:11 says, "Therefore encourage one another and build each other up, just as in fact you are doing." In this chapter, Paul is writing from a jail cell to the people of Thessalonica to remind them of how he lived among them and more importantly, reaffirm that they are to support each other and work toward the call of Christ. Paul marinates on how to address these people and responds with consideration and compassion. This is an example of why it's important to process thoroughly, then respond.

TRUST THE PROCESS

Okay, so if you are in this room, you have spent enough time together to know something about your mate that you don't like. If you can't think of even one thing you don't particularly care for about your mate, you should leave immediately! You haven't spent enough time together and you haven't gotten to know each other well enough. (I'm kidding... sort of!)

Let's take ten minutes—five minutes per person—and tell your mate, your boo, your sweetie, one thing that you don't like that they do, they say, whatever. Share something you don't like about them.

For the mate who has just received this wonderful information, I don't want you to immediately respond. I want you to take thirty seconds to process the comments. Look at a clock. Don't respond for thirty seconds. Concentrate on breathing as you marinate and process.

Do you see the validity in their statement? Is this something you can change? Is this something you want to change? Even if you don't want to change or it will be hard, is the sacrifice good for the benefit of the marriage? Is your mate more important than your lack of desire to change? Is this thing ultimately a deal breaker on either side of the relationship? These are just some of the questions you can ponder in these thirty seconds.

Spend ten to twenty minutes discussing this exercise in class. Ask yourself if you listened to your mate. Did you focus on what they were saying without waiting to talk? Did you really take the thirty seconds to marinate on what they said and then respond with consideration for their needs and how they feel?

The discussion piece is important, but self-evaluation in this exercise is crucial. Your mate, more than anyone in the world, wants you to hear them. Your ear, your thoughts, and your response in general will mean more to him/her than anyone else in the world. Think about that for a moment. How you respond to most of what your spouse will share with you means more than anything anyone else says! I think we sometimes lose this recognition in the black community because we have so many distractions from friends, to relatives, to reality tv. The list goes on and on of how many people and things we interact with on a daily basis. That said, in a marriage which is healthy and growing every day, the most important response on earth in marriage is how your respond to your mate. Listen with empathy, respond with love each and every time.

Chapter Four

"That's *Your* Child!"

Blended Families

A reality of living in this era is there are a lot of blended families being created, especially in the black community. Results from the Pew Research Center in 2011[1] showed that almost one in four black men (24%) had a stepchild. The same study showed that 14% of black women also had a stepchild. Looking deeper into this research, black men are more likely than white men (15%) or Hispanic men (7%) to have stepchildren. The fact of the matter is, our community—at a higher rate than others—marries into families with children from a previous relationship. We must understand that when we choose this path, it isn't easy, but it's necessary to work diligently every single day to make the "family" be more important than the fact this particular family is "blended."

I'll address some of the reasons for why the black community has more blended families later in the guidebook, but now I want to begin the journey around how to manage your blended families.

---

[1] https://www.pewsocialtrends.org/2011/01/13/a-portrait-of-stepfamilies/

Taking Responsibility

One of the biggest challenges in beginning to manage a newly blended family is the fact that we have to accept responsibility for where we are and how we got here. A prime example of these issues and quite frankly, saddest, commentaries I see in relationships where there are blended families is the bitterness and lack of willingness to take responsibility of the previously failed marriage or relationship. You see, healing the relationship between parents to a level of being able to make mature decisions where they can align their own wants and needs with the needs of the child is where it all starts. Getting to this point starts with taking accountability. If you or your soon-to-be spouse is struggling with co-parenting with the parent from a previous relationship, let's do these four things:

 Set up a meeting with the other parent. Take responsibility for what happened. There's too much to try to sort out everything and place blame for one thing and say "my fault" for another. Simply take responsibility and say: "I could have done this differently and I didn't. I'm holding myself responsible and accountable for the situation." Which brings me to the next point...

 Apologize. Not a half-hearted, insincere apology. You don't have to grovel, either. Be honest. Apologize and say you are sorry for where you went wrong (not for how they took it—no backhanded, pseudo-apologies!). The most important thing here is to be sincere.

 Patience. Please understand your ability to move on may not be the exact same timeframe for them. Give them time and space. Be mature about the situation but be patient. You didn't get here overnight, you can't fix it overnight. Especially in extremely challenging situations, take baby steps. Give them time to start to work with you and get on the same page one day at a time, one step at a time.

Honor. I think it is highly important to honor both your child's biological parent and your new partner in this situation. It also takes a very high level of maturity in what could be an intimidating situation. Honor the biological parent as they play an important part in your child's development. They are going to be around for the duration of the relationship with your child. Speak highly of them to your child and never speak ill of them.

Just as importantly, honor your new spouse in these situations. Your biological co-parent may have some raw feelings and emotions right now. Treat them with compassion, but be honest, yet tactful about the fact your spouse is going to be a part of your child's life. The bio parent and your spouse need to also be on the same page. I think of actor Jada Pinkett-Smith and Sheree Fletcher (Will Smith's ex-wife). They struggled to develop a relationship, but with work and persistence they were able to get on the same page. Will honored both women in their children's lives and I think that was key in developing the relationship they have today.

Integration

Okay, so we've taken the huge step of taking responsibility for our actions. Now, how do we move forward? We have to make plans to integrate our lives. Literally, blend our family dynamics. Sometimes this is difficult, but it is necessary, and, with work, it can be done.

As you grow with your spouse, you will find you each have different backgrounds, different upbringings. What you may not have considered is that your upbringings actually developed your parenting style. How you lead your children is a direct correlation to how you were reared. This is important to understand because each of us were raised in a different environment in different styles. Now, we must integrate our style to raise our children, biological or blended. How do we do this? Here's a few ways to develop a plan.

Discussion

When we have a topic that applies to the children, address those topics privately first. Let's come to a consensus on the decision we want to make. This isn't always as easy as it sounds. It may require negotiation, compromise, and consideration. The important thing is to talk it though and get on the same page to bring a united front to the child. It's not an "us vs them" thing, it's parents delivering their child the best option for a particular situation. This is important in all families, but I think it's even more paramount in blended families. Being united is the key to successful parenting in blended families.

Follow Through

Being in a blended family myself, I'm guilty of not following through to the level my wife requires in parenting from time to time. We may ask our daughter to do something, she doesn't follow through to a certain level of expectation and I'm a bit more lenient than I should be. We have to follow through on our expectations as blended families. We will send mixed messages to children if we have one parent that requires a certain expectation and one that doesn't. It's easy for a child to gravitate toward one parent or another— generally the one who is more lenient. We have to keep a united mindset and hold our children accountable to their expectations.

My pastor once said, "We're not raising children, we're raising adults." I don't think truer words have been spoken. We are developing young minds to learn responsibility and accountability. When we don't hold them to that standard and they go out into the world, we can expect them to do exactly what they have practiced. Not being accountable and responsible at school, on the job, at church or at home. It is our responsibility to require them to meet the expectation we set for them—and to be united in doing so.

Consequences and Discipline

Each family should come up with their own rules and regulations around discipline. Please understand nothing is set in stone and there are going to be many different ways to look at discipline. We must also understand that what worked for one child may not work for another. Parents must be flexible enough to try to figure out what discipline gets the desired results. Proverbs 13:24 says, "Whoever spares the rod hates their children, but the one who loves their children is careful to discipline them." The important thing to remember about discipline is that God disciplines us as His children as well. He disciplines us to sharpen us. It makes us better. The Amplified Bible takes Proverbs 13:24 farther and says "...but he who loves him disciplines and trains him diligently and appropriately (with wisdom and love)." Discipline feels like it sucks in the moment, whether you are giving it or receiving it. The ultimate result of the discipline far outweighs the consequence of discipline in the moment. Agree on discipline for your children. Stick to the discipline. Give the consequence with wisdom and love. It will serve them well all of their lives.

Celebration and Recognition

As important as it is to discipline our children, I believe it is just as important to celebrate them and recognize their accomplishments. Have genuine discussions with them about how they are doing in school or in extra-curricular activities. When they do well, recognize it. When they do their best, celebrate it! My candid thought is that our world is probably giving too many participation trophies, which is creating an atrophy in our desire to be the best. That's not what I'm talking about here. We don't need to celebrate the fact you get up and go to school every day, which is your minimum requirement. What we can celebrate is that you have been selected for the math team, when your poorest subject was math and you applied yourself. Let's celebrate being third place in a race considering when you started the season you could barely finish the race at all. Let's celebrate and recognize our children's striving for greatness. Children will respond to being honored and recognized by their parents. I don't think I have ever seen a bigger smile on my daughter's face than when my wife was talking to her family about how far my daughter had come in running the 100m dash from the start of the track season to the end. She was so happy that she had gotten recognition—ironically, in front of her blended family.

You notice I titled the chapter: "That's your child!" Every parent has been frustrated enough, whether blended family or otherwise to say or think "That is your child; I'm not dealing with this right now." It's natural. Children can be frustrating. Be honest with yourself and your emotions. Holding it in doesn't help anyone. That said, be considerate when sharing your thoughts. Take a walk. Let the pressure of parenting diminish. Make sure and take vacations without the children. Your health, mentally and otherwise, is important to help children develop. Deal with the pressure of parenting in a healthy way. Relax and unwind so you can come back to the children with a fresh new attitude.

When you keep your attitude revitalized you can think clearer. You can make decisions that are in the child's best interest. You can give guidance and direction, consequence and discipline from a place of love and genuine care rather than frustration and anger.

Two final points about blended families:

Caring

You must communicate sincerely that you care. You care about your bonus child. You care about your mate's situation with the bio parent. You care about how the bio parent feels about the situation. It is said people care about what you know, when they know that you care. When you are trying to get a point across to a child, they need to know first that you care. When you are trying to help your spouse work through a tough situation in the blended family construct, your mate must know that you care.

Commitment

My awesome wife told me when we got married that she was all-in on my daughter. This meant she was all-in on school, all-in on hygiene, all-in on teaching her what moms should teach daughters, all-in on talking about boys, all-in on discipline, all-in on recognition, all-in on preparing her for college and life and all-in on loving her unconditionally and being the best mom possible. My wife is all-in on all of it! She has been nothing but awesome with our daughter for the duration of our relationship. Now, none of us are perfect, but use my wife's example to consider: Being committed and drawing a line in the sand that nothing will break this commitment is a key to showing how much you care. You have to take it all on. The good, the bad, the ugly—all of it. Say it in front of the child, that you are committed. No matter how much you go through, the family is going to stick it out together. The child will never forget it and it will deepen the relationship.

EXERCISE

COMMITMENT

The exercise for this lesson is to talk about what taking responsibility looks like. How do we integrate our lives?

What does discussion around responsibility in blended families sound like? Has anyone in the group experienced it and want to share? Explain what follow through looks like to you. Talk to the group about both challenges and successes when it comes to consequences and discipline. Give some examples. Also, give a few examples of what celebration and recognition looks like and when it is appropriate.

Finally, let's have a few couples explain what caring and commitment looks and feels like to them. Encourage the couples to take good notes. This is a good chapter to look back on during the marriage.

Chapter Five

I'm sick and tired of being sick and tired. Do it again and see what happens...

Learning how to resolve conflict without sarcasm, dares, and ultimatums

Let's make one guarantee from the outset: Conflict will happen in marriage. It's not if, it's when, and let's add on "how often" for good measure. Different people from different backgrounds with different sets of ideas and mindsets are bound to disagree. Even if you're buzzing along in pre-marital bliss, trust me, it's going to happen. The question is, how do we deal with it when it comes up, how do we process conflict and how do we resolve it.

Before I touch on the components of acknowledging conflict, processing conflict and resolving conflict, let's establish one foundational component of conflict resolution:

Not Optional

DIVORCE IS OFF THE TABLE. IT'S A NON-STARTER. NON-NEGOTIABLE.

Let's make it clear how important this point is. Let's assume you find a house you would like to buy. The seller has it listed for $300,000.00. You can't afford $300,000, but you want the house. You offer $175.000.00. You write a letter of why you want this particular house; how much you would love it and take care of it. What you don't know is that the seller is buying another home for $400k and they have to get $300k to pay off their home and have a sufficient down payment to move. Your offer is not accepted. Not only is it not accepted, they don't even take the time to reply. It's a non-starter. The seller won't even have a conversation with you starting at $175k.

This is how both parties must look at divorce. Malachi 2:16 NIV says, "'The man who hates and divorces his wife,' says the Lord, the God of Israel, 'does violence to the one he should protect,' says the Lord Almighty." Think about this for a moment. The man who divorces his wife actually does violence to the one he should protect.

Husbands, when you take this woman to be your lawfully wedded wife, you promise to protect her with everything you have for the rest of your life. That's really what this guidebook is about. Be sure and confident in your decision of who you are marrying, because she is your responsibility forever. Conflict will arise. She is your responsibility. Betrayal, disloyalty, grief, sickness, financial loss, changes of heart and the list goes on may arise in your marriage. I pray it does not, but if it does, husbands, she is your responsibility. You have to take divorce off the table. Once you take it away, you will find something you haven't considered. You can make it through anything. You can survive and thrive through anything.

Wives, you must be the solid rock of the marriage. Taking another page from my lovely wife, she told me when we got married "Please understand, we are not getting divorced. It's not optional. We'll fight through whatever problems we have. We'll argue, we may even be upset with each other for a season. But divorce is not an option. We're getting married, but we must have that understanding." I never forgot those words. She took divorce off the table before we could even consider it. This is my requirement of you. More importantly, make this YOUR requirement of yourself first and of your spouse secondarily. When you make this decision of marriage and vow your lives together to become one flesh by God joining you together, you have also, by default, eliminated divorce from the equation. Keep in mind, divorce is a human construct approved by people. Marriage is a divine construct, approved by God himself.

Before we leave this topic, let's briefly discuss. This takes some courage. We need your honesty; this is how we learn from each other and grow.

Who in the room believes divorce is an option?

Why?

Does the scripture I have quoted (and others) revise your thinking on divorce?

Why or why not?

Finally, is God's Word the final Word on divorce?

Why or why not?

Acknowledging Conflict

Many people struggle with acknowledging conflict. Some of us go into our shell. We just don't want to deal with it. Let's be clear, the longer you allow it to simmer, the worse it becomes for both parties. We have to make a conscious choice to deal with things when they appear.

Some of us are the extreme to the other end of the spectrum. We acknowledge the conflict so much it consumes us. Our emotions get the best of us and we can't function until we get the problem resolved. This isn't healthy either. We must find a balance to understand that most conflict takes time to develop and most will also take time to resolve. Let's try an exercise to find out exactly how we generally acknowledge conflict:

ACKNOWLEDGING CONFLICT

At this point, you should know your mate well enough to know what they like, don't like, what really ticks them off and what pushes their buttons a little. This is the one and only time for the next fifty years that you are going to be allowed to push their buttons!

This is a fun role play. Dive into your character to make this work. You are playing...yourself! Wives, think of something your husband doesn't like, doesn't do well or it simply irks him. I want you to tell him something that would get a rise out of him. Husbands, all I want you to do is respond as though the situation was real. Easy enough—just be yourself.

After about ten minutes, let's flip it. Husbands to be, I'm going to guess you can nail this one. Think of something your mate doesn't like—maybe it's something you do or don't do (for me, it might be leaving socks on the floor—I plead the fifth!). Whatever that thing is that gets her fired up, talk about it. Wives, give your normal response. At the end of each, the mate who "started the problem" I want you to listen to your mate's response and see which of these your mate exemplifies in their response.

What we learn from this exercise is what your natural inclination is when conflict arises. Do you use a fight or flight technique? Do you generally lean toward becoming defensive? Do you make excuses or explanations? Do you listen and respond accordingly or are you inclined to jump in with a solution? None of these are necessarily wrong in and of themselves, they are simply how you are predisposed to reacting to conflict.

We can all grow and get better when dealing with our natural inclination toward conflict. Now that you know your natural inclinations (you will likely have more than one), you can think about how to acknowledge conflict in a way that is healthy for your marriage. Every person is going to have different things to work on here. For example: if you naturally want to go to the silent treatment because you don't want to deal with issues head on, for the benefit of the marriage and resolving conflict in a timely manner, you will want to start to communicate about an issue even when it is uncomfortable. It's pulling you out of your comfort zone—I know! I'm an introvert that happens to be a public speaker. I get pulled out of my comfort zone every time I'm on stage or in front of a camera. Once, I even knocked over a microphone stand on stage in front of about 800 people! I had to get back on that stage later that night. Heaven knows, I didn't want to, but I did.

You have to make yourself come out of your comfort zone to fight unhealthy inclinations. Keep doing it. It will help you grow to acknowledge things properly and more importantly work through problems quicker. When you learn how to acknowledge problems in a healthy way, the process and resolution happens faster and usually with less pain. You make the problem become more of a simple inconvenience.

EXERCISE   DATE: _____

RESOLVING CONFLICT

Let's do another exercise tonight. Write down two things you can do to resist your natural inclination to be more thoughtful in processing and resolving conflict in your marriage.

_____

_____

_____

Processing Conflict

One may think processing and acknowledging conflict is the same thing, but it is not. Acknowledgement is the initial acceptance and response to an issue. Processing the issue is putting in the work to resolve an issue.

Marriages do not work on autopilot, nor are they a dictatorship with one person making every decision. Marriage is partnership at the highest level. You will find in healthy marriages most issues are not resolved by compromise. Most conflicts are resolved through cooperation and consideration to make the best decision for everyone involved. Compromise suggests both people give some type of concession to decide on a conclusion agreeable for everyone. The truth is, when compromise happens, neither party generally gets what they want and no one leaves happy.

When processing conflict, keep this in mind: You want to work together to get to the best resolution for the marriage. Try to find out the most important need for everyone involved. Keep asking needs when processing. Looking at an example like where we want to live, I may ask, why a certain location is important. What is most important about that location to you? How important is location A versus location B to you? If you could have three things in this move to another location, what would they be?

When you start asking questions, you often find that things we assume matter, don't matter at all. Using this scenario, you may find you think someone wants to be close to work, but they really want to avoid traffic and another location may be better.

The process of resolving conflict is the most important component when dealing with conflict. The reason it is the most important is that the process shows how much you care about your mate. You want to be considerate when processing conflict. This doesn't mean you become a doormat or your wants or needs don't matter, but this goes back to selfishness vs selflessness. When you get married, his or her needs come first. Process with a selfless heart. The awesomeness in processing with a selfless heart is that you are almost fighting for your mate's position on behalf of them. It gives you enlightenment into their perspective.

Conflict in our community often comes from the disparity in socioeconomic backgrounds. What one thinks is extravagant, another believes is normal—and needed. When we process considerations like private school, luxury cars, living in one neighborhood vs another, etc., we need to be considerate of a person's mindset. You may have to explain your case of why you want to send the kids to this school or you want to get your weekly mani/pedi/massage. You may have to explain why this two-seater sports car makes sense (I hope my wife reads this part...lol!). Impasses in processing problem solving and conflict resolution often in the black community are often not about the conflict itself, but about how you think about money and material things. It is often residue of your background and your expectation of how to deal with money. This isn't the case for each and every conflict in marriage, but many of these conflicts can be avoided by having conversations to learn the mindset of your partner around money, and share your expectations around financial issues as well. Be considerate and tactful in those conversations as well. We want to grow and process conflict the right way, but we want to do it in a loving, compassionate way.

Resolving Conflict

You've done the hard part, now it's simply making a decision—or is it that simple? What you are going to find more often than not is there is not one clear, agreeable solution. It will happen sometimes, but most of the time, there will be options. Easy challenges have easy decisions. Conflicts and tough challenges generally have options that open paths. You and your mate have to select the path to follow. I heard President Obama say that the decisions that reach his desk are all hard, the easy ones have been answered before they get to him. You will find that to be the case sometimes, as the CEO and COO of your marriage.

The most important point here is to actually make the decision to resolve the conflict. Making no decision is the equivalent of making a decision to do nothing. Conflict doesn't resolve itself. You have to take a pro-active, interactive part in getting things to change.

After you have processed the conflict, you are generally left with options. It sounds simple, but the goal is to select the best option. Unfortunately, there is no option angel out there that lands on your shoulder and says, "B is the best option—roll with that one." You have to take the information you have, use your wisdom and discernment and make a decision. If it's a decision on something like going to therapy for your marriage or fighting through it on your own, take the info you have, weigh it out, pray about it (and everything related to your marriage) and make the decision and move on. I see some couples get paralysis by analysis and simply are stuck because they can't decide which path to take. Take the one you believe is best—remembering that divorce is not an option—and move forward with the intent to make your marriage stronger and better.

One thing that helps in resolving conflict is remembering there are no bad decisions. You have heard there are no stupid questions. The reason for that statement is something that doesn't make sense to you could make a lot of sense to another person, because you may be better informed than the other person. It's the same in decision making. There are no stupid decisions. There are choices with consequences. Learning from the consequences helps you in your journey. Make a decision and accept the consequences. A well-thought out decision that doesn't achieve the outcome you want still gives you experience to make better decisions in the future. Resolving conflict requires the C-suite in the marriage to make an executive decision with their collective wisdom and discernment, then move forward.

Unified Front

Resolution in marriage is a joint effort. You must be unified with your mate in conflict resolution. Notice, I didn't say you have to agree on every point. You may disagree on one or more points, but you may see through the process how the decision you and your mate have come to may ultimately provide the best outcome for your marriage. Sometimes, the wife will take the backseat on a topic and allow her husband to lead. Sometimes, the husband, in his infinite wisdom (wives, y'all can at least let us believe that) will understand his wife's perspective is the best way to resolve a conflict and he will totally accept her resolution. Whatever the case, unified resolutions that come from a selfless heart and have been processed by both people in the marriage yield the best results.

EXERCISE

DATE: _____

UNIFIED FRONT

The exercise for conflict resolution is homework. I would like you to send me a note to the email address I provide with the first conflict you resolve together after you are married. It can be big or small or anything in-between. I'm excited to find out how each of you resolves conflict! Don't forget about us; we'll be checking in.

Chapter Six

No Excuses. No Explanations

Everyone takes ownership, accountability,
and responsibility for challenges

You'll find this topic is everywhere in the book. It is inherent to what we need to do daily in our lives. The thing we miss is that we are responsible, personally for everything that happens to us. We can't control everything that happens in our environment. Some things can happen "to" you that you can't control. You can always control your response. You can always take responsibility for your response.

I adopted this motto as the theme for our house. No excuses, no explanations. What does that really mean? If I were writing a retort to this chapter, I would call it "Blame, Here's why."

I first heard this phrase from NFL coach, Jason Garrett. He used it as a motto with his team. It was posted on the walls in the locker room. He said it during meetings and practices. It was really enlightening to me. We often place blame on circumstances. Look at it from a football perspective. Players get injured. Players get suspended. Players retire. We don't have the same system. We don't have players that fit the system we have in place. We don't have enough experience at quarterback. None of it matters when you really get down to it. All of those things are explanations. In the case of Garrett's team, the year he used this motto, they were legitimate explanations. It. Does. Not. Matter. Your set of circumstances are what they are. You must play the hand you are dealt to the best of your ability. Effort is fine, but results are what history records. What results can you produce? This is what it means when we say, "no excuses, no explanations." What do your results look like?

Personal responsibility in marriage in the black community is even more important than in other communities. You're probably thinking, "Why would he write that?" Because it's true. We have been dealt a bad hand socio-economically. We have drawn the short straw when it comes to how black men have been affected historically in this country, which has led to the higher number of single parent homes in the black community. We have to walk the streets like we carry a scarlet letter when we encounter police. It is said that some communities have a certain level of privilege. Let's be honest, our community has an equal and opposite disadvantage to that privilege. It is wise to acknowledge reality, however, allow me to be crystal clear. It. Does. Not. Matter. Explanations can explain why your marriage doesn't thrive, why a spouse cheats on their spouse, why we run to divorce as an option, but it doesn't change the fact that the marriage is failing—on your watch!

Allow me to share a quick story about responsibility before we dive into what it looks like for your marriage. I often attended a men's meeting to discuss issues and work on growing together. It was kind of a small group. It was incredibly helpful. Men sharpening each other as iron sharpens iron. We added an individual who was clearly intelligent, understood our plight as a community and also understood that women were a gift to us and he was grateful for his wife. There was one challenge. Each time we would meet, he would come and explain how "the white man" had done something to set him back. Most often, it was how he was set back in his profession. Each time, it was a venting session and more and more about what "the white man" did to hold him back and oppress our community. Again, some of the things he said were not debatable. The problem is, he wasn't offering solutions on how to move forward. He wasn't giving alternatives or initiatives to make his situation better or his community better. It was excuses and explanations. I always pushed back on finding solutions. Eventually, unfortunately, he stopped coming. I believe it was unfortunate because he was very intelligent and could have made an incredible contribution to the community, but he wouldn't get out of his own way. I would have liked to see him discover the burden, yet power of taking responsibility for himself and his community, to positively impact the world.

Ownership

Your marriage belongs to you. It's no one else's responsibility. It's God's responsibility to provide direction and make your crooked places straight. The rest of it, that's on you, boo. Bruh, you got it. Not your spouse, not your mom, not your dad, not your girlfriend who is giving you bad advice that isn't working on her own relationship. This one is on you. As I mentioned above, it is a burden, but there is power in responsibility.

In the first marriage, excuses and explanations got us right where we are today. Adam blamed Eve for giving him the forbidden fruit and he blamed God for giving him the woman. Your boy apparently had nothing to do with receiving the fruit and eating it. It's "everyone else's fault." His lack of responsibility is a big part of the fallen world as we know it. Use this information to remind you to continually take responsibility for your marriage.

Marriage is a lot of things. It's a big deal. It's serious. It's fun. It's a commitment. It's shared pain. It's shared parenting. It's shared responsibility. It's worship together. It's sharing love for each other. Most importantly, it's yours. You have to take care of the marriage. Taking care of your spouse is important, but let's think of how to take ownership of the marriage.

Let's try a group exercise on ownership.

EXERCISE

DATE:

OWNERSHIP

Let's assume for a moment you owned a coffee shop. I want your group to write down ten things that are important to owning this shop. Stop at ten. Your facilitator is going to put your ten things on the whiteboard. The groups are going to vote on the list from each group. The group voted with the best coffee shop ownership will each win $5.00 Starbucks gift cards.

- Customer Service
- Quality Product / Consistency
- Diversity
- Well-trained Staffed
- Code of Conduct / Mission Statement / Vision
- Finance Accountant
- Marketing / Promotion
- Cleanliness
- Hours of Operation
- location

Staying Engaged

We discussed what ownership means in a marriage, meaning everything that happens is your responsibility. That said, how do you make sure you are in a place to take ownership of your marriage and your life? The answer is to stay engaged in what is going on. You might be surprised how people do not engage in their marriages. Some people get frustrated and check out. Some people simply expect (*assume* is probably a better word) their spouse to take care of things. It could be bills, children, housing, any number of things. Many times, someone will stay out of a lot of what is going on in the marriage. You have to make the decision to stay engaged. It doesn't mean you are making every decision. It does mean that you are aware of what is going on, it matters to you and you work on it together. Every couple will have different ways of decision making. Much of that will come from how each of you were raised.

Regardless of how you were raised, this book is here to remind you that you have to make a conscious decision every morning to stay engaged in your marriage. If you don't pay the bills, find out when they are due, what needs to be paid, and how much. You could remind your spouse in a pinch or even step in and pay a few bills if necessary. Another example of staying engaged is the fact that even though I happen to do the laundry in our home, my wife knows how to use this twenty-first century, wi-fi enabled, washer (does a washer really need wi-fi? I digress...) if need be. She makes it her business to stay engaged.

Rolling with the Punches

I have news for you. There will be punches in your marriage. Punches from family, friends, co-workers, people you don't know, bill collectors, your boss, your mechanic, your contractor, your doctor, your children, your neighbors, your government, your court system, your tax collector, etc. You will be punched. Some are jabs, some are right hooks, some are devastating upper cuts. You will find many of these punches will be glancing blows, maybe a scare with your doctor, or getting a raise, but not what you were expecting. Some will be right on the button, possibly a miscarriage or loss of a job and you just have one income. This is a bit of a harsh reality, but you have to be aware, life will happen, to each and every one of us.

Floyd "Money" Mayweather and Thomas "Hitman" Hearns are two great Welterweight champions. Different styles of boxers, but both great in their own right. Hearns may have had the best punch in his day. Floyd was a defensive tactician with quick hands. Hearns' record was 61 wins, 5 losses and 1 draw. Mayweather's record is 50 wins with 0 losses. The biggest difference? Floyd knew how to take a punch and roll with the punches. Literally. He had a certain type of defense that protected his chin and he had a beautiful shoulder roll to keep form absorbing punishment. Hearns landed a lot, but he was hit on the "button" often. He didn't know how to roll with the punches. That's what you must learn to weather the storms of marriage and take responsibility in the process. How do you roll with the punches?

The first thing in marriage we have to do is quickly acknowledge this is a blow. Whatever the problem, issue, tragedy, accept this is what we have to deal with it. The more quickly you accept this external issue, the more quickly we can figure out how to take it. Think about this example: What if your house was to go into foreclosure? What is the first thing you do? Do you panic? Do you start to pack? What do you do?

Whatever the situation, take a breath. Analyze the situation. Remember, excuses and explanations don't matter. Using this scenario, what matters right now is a roof over our head and making sure our family is taken care of. This is how you roll with the punches. Stick it out, together. Talk through it. Develop a plan and move on it. Husbands, lead when you have to make tough decisions and be responsible and accountable. Wives, support your husband, whether the decision works out perfectly or whether it could have had a better outcome.

If the house goes into foreclosure, and you save it, great. You took responsibility, created a plan of action and it worked out. If the house is foreclosed on and you can't save it, the punch stings a little more, but you still have to live. You will. You will survive. You will thrive! You still develop a plan, even though it's a plan B. Follow the plan and do what you need to do to keep your family safe and healthy. Plans require adjustments. You two work together and make the necessary adjustments. Get in a stable situation and take a breath. It's only for a moment. The punch tried to take you out, but what it did is it made you learn more. It prepared you for your next home ownership.

It put you in a better position to succeed going forward. No excuses, no explanation necessary. Took the punch, kept it moving.

Mindset

Lastly, taking responsibility for your actions and the health of your marriage largely depends on how you think of the idea of responsibility and accountability. We can teach you to listen, if you are open to become a better listener. We can teach you to become more understanding, if you care for your spouse and you know understanding is going to be important to making everyday a good day. Responsibility is different. The world shuns responsibility daily. We see images on TV and the internet daily of people who could have an incredible impact on the world who place blame and take zero accountability for their actions. Pastor Rick Warren said in a sermon series, "What you blame, you empower." If you blame your student loans for your financial situation, you empower money. If you blame your job for your lack of career advancement, you empower your job. Back to the story of the first couple, Eve blamed the serpent. Eve empowered the serpent by blaming him.

Mindset is your attitude and perspective on a given situation or set of circumstances. My mindset on my marriage is that the marriage and everything attached to it is my responsibility. Good, bad or indifferent. It falls on me. This mindset takes courage. It takes prayer and faith. It takes belief that the institution of marriage is the best thing in my life and every day we make it better. It's on me to make that happen. If you were to ask my wife, she would tell you it is on her to make it happen. We are all-in, 100%, mentally and psychologically to our responsibility, and accountability to this marriage and to each other. This may sound a bit like hyperbole, but it's not. It can't be hyperbole for you and your spouse either. Make the only decision to make this marriage work: Today, shift your mind to the fact that you two are in this together, committed, regardless of circumstances or consequences to see this through until you meet again in Heaven. When you choose this mindset, you choose your marriage above everything else in this world and nothing in this world can stop the success and healthy state of your marriage. Your bond will truly be unbreakable.

EXERCISE

MINDSET

Write a paragraph (twenty-five words or so) about what you believe responsibility to your marriage looks like. If you need a few more words feel free. Write it in this guidebook. Go back to it when you need a reminder. When you finish writing the paragraph, I want you to read it aloud to your mate. Look at them and let them know you choose to be responsible for the union you are about to enter into.

Chapter Seven

I'm Dealing with Some Stuff—I Need Your Support

Learning to ask for help with abuse, addiction & post-traumatic stress—and being willing to offer support when asked

This is one of the biggest reasons we developed this program. Our community, your community, the black community, doesn't deal with our trauma nearly enough. It's getting better, but we are still underserved. There are shows on TV with people who look like us talking to therapists and counselors. There are celebrities beginning to talk about the fact they are dealing with mental and psychological trauma and they are working through it with therapy and coaching. The reality is real people living lives not in the public eye don't deal with our internal issues that impact our day to day psyche nearly enough. If you want your marriage to work—and I know you do, or you wouldn't be here—you have to do this work. This is life-changing stuff if you will dig into this chapter and do the follow-on work.

Abuse

Abuse comes in many forms. Physical abuse is the most common form we consider. There is mental abuse, verbal abuse, emotional abuse, and even psychological abuse. Psychological abuse has to do with how to control someone by taking advantage of their situation and manipulating their mind. Psychological abuse is one of the toughest forms of abuse to overcome in relationships because there is no one-size-fits-all remedy to remove one's self from psychological abuse. Simply leaving isn't enough. We will dig deeper, but let's continue the overview.

This is a pre-marital course. Prior to marriage, we need to understand what we are getting ourselves into. Before marriage, we also need to be aware of the abuse we have suffered in childhood, adolescence, adulthood, and in previous relationships. One of the definitions of abuse is "to treat (a person or an animal) with cruelty or violence, especially regularly or repeatedly." When you think of the depth of abuse, it literally means someone has treated you with cruelty over and over again. There is a toll on your mind and body that comes with abuse. You have to deal with it. We repress our thoughts and feelings to cope and make it through life. Coping mechanisms allow us to survive, but marriages are our opportunity to thrive. Let's consider some tools to take control of how abuse has impacted our thinking.

Confront the Issue

It's hard to accept, but before you walk into this marriage you have to be real with yourself and accept that you have been a victim of abuse. You must realize this isn't a self-inflicted wound and someone treated you in a way you didn't deserve to be treated. It's okay to realize you have been a victim. It's also important to realize you are no longer a victim and you don't accept a victim's mentality. You accept that you were in a bad relationship or you had parents that didn't know how to treat you, but your mere presence doesn't make you a co-conspirator in your own abuse. Today is the day you want to confront the issue. Within your own mind. In your heart. Make a decision. Acknowledgement and acceptance are the first components in dealing with abuse. You're going into a marriage with someone who loves you and has your best interest at heart. Let's talk about next steps when dealing with abuse. This is where your partner comes in.

EXERCISE

CONFRONTATION AND TAKING CONTROL

Before we move on, we want to do an exercise. This is an individual exercise for a party of one. For each individual who feels like they have some abuse or trauma they need to address, I want to pause to do some work here. The hardest part for some (not all) of dealing with abuse is the acknowledgement. We want to forget it. We want to repress it. We want to ignore it or act like it never happened. You can't resolve it that way. This is a simple exercise. Take out some paper. Don't type this. Don't think about this and consider the exercise done—it's not. Write down the fact that you were abused, addicted or traumatized. You don't need to go into the details of the act or acts but put it on paper and write what kind of trauma it was (mental, emotional, physical, psychological, verbal or in some form I have not listed).

On the next line, give yourself one or two sentences to explain that it wasn't your fault. Explain to yourself why it wasn't your fault. You had no control, for example. You were a child, you were in a controlling relationship. Whatever the reason it was not your fault, write it down. Acknowledge to yourself on paper for you to see that the abuse was not on you. Finally, tell yourself on paper that you are not a victim and you will not have a victim's mentality. More importantly, write down one or two reasons why you will not have a victim's mentality.

Keep this note. It's not for anyone else's consumption. Read it. Put it away. Refer back to it on tough days. Refer back to it as you are doing the work, and it seems like the work isn't helping. Work isn't easy, it isn't fast, and sometimes takes significant time to make progress. That said, you can always pull out this note to remind you it's worth it. You're worth it. This little note can be your way of providing yourself comfort when you need it most.

Support

Asking for support isn't always easy. Especially when you have struggled confronting this weight you have been dealing with. Find people you can confide in. If you're getting married to someone you want to spend the rest of your life with, I'm going to encourage you to be vulnerable. They need to know your challenges and they need to know about your abuse. If you need their support, let them know. You should expect them to be there for you.

Here's a reality check: Your mate could run from the situation. If so, it's the best news you could have gotten. If they run from supporting you in dealing with this past abuse, they will run when times get tough down the road. You need to know that information before marriage. Most importantly, you need support to take the next steps. You need your partner to be there for you as you walk this tough journey of healing.

Support is also going to come in the form of a therapist. You will want to find a therapist who can help with the specific abuse you have dealt with. Often, specific counselors have dealt more with some problems than others. Look for someone who has dealt with your set of issues. Check for referrals, look for people who can help you work through the trauma. The important thing to remember is that there is a better life on the other side of this journey. Be willing to walk this journey out and show your mate you plan to do your best to be healthy to start your marriage.

Let me also be clear to say that every mate isn't a counselor, coach, or therapist. Every person isn't going to be the right person to talk to about your issues. Also, some individuals don't have the capability to give the proper advice or insight regarding things like abuse, addiction or post-traumatic stress. Please be aware of that when you're talking to your mate. It is reasonable to believe that your mate's support can come in the level of compassion, the listening ear and the amount of comfort that you need to feel supported through this challenging time. Don't put the expectation that you see in another marriage or relationship on your mate, especially when it comes to something like this. Allow your mate to be the best version of themselves and support you in the way that you need them, yet in a way they can be good for you.

Addiction

The ugly truth is addiction happens at a higher rate in the black community than the national average. According to the U.S. Department of Health and Human Services, the rate of illegal drug use in 2014 was 12.4% for

African Americans compared to the national average of 10.2%.[2] In a country of approximately 44.5 million African Americans, this means we have approximately 5.4 million of us engaging in illegal drug use. A little better than one in ten of us. What this means is that likely, in your family, you have someone who is addicted or has been addicted to substance abuse. It's a shocking statistic. It should be. We have to address the addiction problem in our community.

The best way for this program to address the addiction problem is to help you acknowledge it in your own homes. We have to own our problem. We have to know the symptoms and then have the selflessness to love our spouse enough to reach out for help. Look at these common symptoms of addiction according to the Mayo Clinic:

 Feeling that you have to use the drug regularly — daily or even several times a day

 Having intense urges for the drug that block out any other thoughts

 Over time, needing more of the drug to get the same effect

 Taking larger amounts of the drug over a longer period of time than you intended

 Making certain that you maintain a supply of the drug

 Spending money on the drug, even though you can't afford it

 Not meeting obligations and work responsibilities, or cutting back on social or recreational activities because of drug use

 Continuing to use the drug, even though you know it's causing problems in your life or causing you physical or psychological harm

 Doing things to get the drug that you normally wouldn't do, such as stealing

[2] Substance Abuse and Mental Health Services Administration, https://www.samhsa.gov/programs

Driving or doing other risky activities when you're under the influence of the drug

 Spending a good deal of time getting the drug, using the drug or recovering from the effects of the drug

 Failing in your attempts to stop using the drug

 Experiencing withdrawal symptoms when you attempt to stop taking the drug

Thirteen examples of symptoms of drug addiction. The challenge I'm setting out to you today is to have a tough conversation with your mate if you see these symptoms in yourself, your mate, or your children to confront addiction.

Again, this is a pre-marital course. If you're dealing with addiction issues with your mate, both of you want to have some level of satisfaction that the addiction is addressed to the extent you can move forward with marriage. This is a hard truth, but a necessary one. Adding marriage to a known addiction is essentially creating more addiction, because now everyone in the family suffers from the addiction of one. Substance abuse is real and if it is not managed properly, it will destroy a new marriage before it starts. Make conscious decisions to manage addiction issues before marriage—both of you will be glad you did.

Assistance from Your Mate

One of the biggest challenges is to figure out how to help the person you love, plan to marry, or have already walked down the aisle with recover from addiction. One of the best places to work through addiction is a center by the name of American Addiction Centers. I would suggest reaching out to them if you need help with substance abuse. There are times you can't reach out to get external help. The best thing you can do is support your mate through the struggle. These are some fantastic tips from American Addiction Centers on how to support your mate struggling with addiction:[3]

 Remember that addiction is not a choice or a moral failing; it is a disease of the brain

 Addiction is ultimately a condition that the individual must learn to manage; no one can take the fight on for the addict.

 Set boundaries and stand by them.

 Encourage the individual to seek help; this may include finding treatment resources for them.

 Find a therapist who specializes in addiction counseling and get help. Loved ones of addicts need support too.

 Set an example for healthy living by giving up recreational drug and alcohol use.

 Be supportive, but do not cover for problems created by substance abuse. The person struggling needs to deal with the consequences of their addiction.

 Be optimistic. A person struggling with drug or alcohol abuse will likely eventually seek help due to ongoing encouragement to do so. If they relapse, it is not a sign of failure; relapse is often part of the overall recovery process.

Relapse

The last bullet point above speaks to the reality that your mate could fall into relapse. If we think of addiction as a disease, we must understand that often diseases are not complete with a one-size-fits-all forever cure. Cancer for

---

[3] Ackerman, Kristina ed. "Loving an Addict or Alcoholic: How to Help them and Yourself." American Addiction Centers, 2019. https://americanaddictioncenters.org/alcoholism-treatment/loving-an-addict.

example sometimes needs to be addressed multiple times to complete treatment. The disease of addiction is no different. Relapse is especially tough for the family because it can look like the patient is cured. Alcoholics Anonymous is correct in the assessment there is no cure for alcoholism. Alcoholics develop tolerance. Opportunity and tolerance can lead to relapse. The challenge of relapse is often a heavier burden again on the family because it's easy to want to give up. One can get the sense of they have done all they can, but the person doesn't want their help.

Remember, this is a disease, not a simple choice. Relapse is a consequence of a disease. Be supportive and optimistic as mentioned above. Working together through relapse continues to show caring and compassion and it is often the support of the spouse that helps the person with the addiction make it through the challenge of relapsing.

Post-Traumatic Stress

One of the disorders we suffer from in the black community the most and discuss the least is called Post-Traumatic Stress Disorder, or more commonly known as PTSD. We think of this when we think about soldiers coming back from war. They have been inundated with the intense stress of war and have not worked through the mental and psychological fatigue that takes a greater toll in many cases than the physical dimension of war. The Mayo Clinic defines PTSD as essentially a condition triggered by a terrifying event while experiencing or witnessing it. For example, first responders often deal with PTSD by the amount of exposure to traumatic events. While we consider the disorder as a medical condition, the reality is in the black community we have been exposed to an inordinate amount of some form of trauma, the cause of post-traumatic stress.

Causes of Post-Traumatic Stress

Something we have learned in this chapter is that abuse, whether subtle or overt is traumatic. Addiction is often a symptom of some other issue in life, but the addiction and the consequences are often traumatic. What we miss in our lives is that we often suffer a traumatic event and we aren't aware in the moment, we're battling traumatic stress later and yet we never really were aware we suffered trauma in the first place. Trauma takes many forms. For example, being moved into foster care or being separated from your family or siblings is traumatic. Grief can be traumatic. Witnessing sexual aggression, homicide, or suicide can be traumatic. Specifically, most of us (black community) suffer from a form of historical trauma where we have been psychologically impaired due to the cultural exploits of the United States historically. As a people, we have generations of suppression and loss to overcome to learn to move forward without the weight of the past being on our shoulders. We feel repressed, yet we accept the repression in some instances because the stress of our trauma has taught what we are about to step into— coping mechanisms.

Coping

The response to stress, whether post-traumatic, job-related, parenting, financial, etc. is always learning how to cope. Coping with stress is essentially how we learn to make it all work. Everyone deals with challenges therefore everyone has to forcibly learn how to cope with them. Each of us have our own coping mechanisms. There are unhealthy coping mechanisms such as substance abuse or disconnecting from family and friends. Look for healthy ways to cope, such as getting a counselor or coach, or getting involved in support groups.

The reason I believe it is important to talk about post-traumatic stress is the fact it is incredibly important to learn how to cope through solid coping skills. Recognize the trauma. Understand how the stress manifests itself in your life. Learn to cope. If we can do these three things, we can manage post-traumatic stress in a way that helps to keep us healthy. Let's talk about ways to manage.

Psychological Evaluation

I can't reiterate enough, you're heading into marriage. This doesn't mean everything will be roses or "fixed," but you will agree with me on the other side of the ring ceremony that it's good that everything is addressed and a work in progress. If you're having flashbacks, memories, nightmares, or physical reactions to something that is bringing you back to an event or situation that was traumatizing to you, it's important to start with an evaluation. You can save yourself years of unwanted pain and unnecessary fear and trepidation with a psychological evaluation. The good news is there is no-one-size-fits-all cure for PTSD. Your care professional will develop the right treatment plan customized for you. Medical professionals can offer different options from medication, cognitive therapy, eye movement desensitization, and other options.

Physical Examination

Often, post-traumatic stress can appear with a physical reaction to a specific event or situation. A common example is a service member who was in a war could hear a car backfire and have a response to this. Although much of PTSD is going to be attributed to how we handle situations with our mind, the physical exam could help with things like rashes or reactions our bodies have to certain experiences and events. When you are working through dealing with PTSD, it's a good idea to have a physical exam for good health and to rule out other issues one could miss with only a psychological evaluation.

Get Plenty of Rest

Our community struggles with getting rest. There's the idea out there that we can "sleep when we die" and we need to "grind" all the time, at all hours, day or night. This is simply untrue. We need rest for our immune systems. We need rest for our brains to work at their full capacity. We need rest to make the best decisions. If you're dealing with stress from trauma, rest will also help with anxiety. Schedule rest. Get the necessary amount of rest for your body, not someone else's. If you need seven hours to feel your best, don't feel bad because your friend is sleeping three hours and "grinding" trying to "make it happen." What they are doing is not respecting their bodies and the lack of rest is working against them, not for them. Get the rest you need and alleviate the stress. Honor what your body is telling you that you need.

The Mayo Clinic and the Department of Health and Human Services have great websites devoted to how to manage Post-Traumatic Stress. If you are looking for other ways to cope, check out these websites. Also, if you are struggling with coping and you are having more serious symptoms such as suicidal thoughts, becoming self-destructive or violent, please seek a therapist immediately, or if it is specifically suicide, please call the National Suicide Prevention Hotline, 1-800-273-TALK (8255).

Conclusion

This is the only chapter with its own conclusion. The reason is we want to drive home the point of being vulnerable, being open to help, understanding you can't be a good husband or wife with the residue of abuse, addiction, or post-traumatic stress permeating throughout your life. Dealing with these things could be the toughest thing you ever do in your life. The flip side of that statement is that dealing with these problems can also be the most satisfying accomplishment of your life. Marriage is an awesome union, but I can promise you that life will set in. Challenges will appear without your help. Life will come at you and your spouse many different ways. One of the best things you can do is deal with abuse on the front end. This way, you know what you are dealing with and how to do so. The residue of abuse, addiction and trauma is like a moth eating away at a dress. It doesn't happen overnight and at first you may not even notice it. As it picks away at the garment, piece by piece, spot by spot, it becomes harder to resolve and the garment is weakened over time. Don't allow you or your relationship to become weaker over time because you don't deal with the pain and abuse now. Get in touch with a counselor, therapist, or coach as soon as possible and move forward building a great life together eliminating the pain of the past.

Chapter Eight

"Babe, I'm here for you, you're not alone"

Working to become proactive in your healing

The one thing in the black community we ignore far more than other communities in America is healing. Healing is intricate to success in any part of life. Healing is a requirement to a successful marriage. Many of us have grown up in situations that are simply not good for our growth, mental health, and in more extreme cases, flat out abusive. We have to own up to the fact we are still living out much of what we dealt with in our younger years. It's especially important to confront the issues we experienced, decide how to get help to work through those issues and then put in the work required to move forward.

How to Fix What You Don't Know is Broken

In relationship coaching, the thing I hear the most is one mate blaming the other for something. It's probably not surprising that very few people initially take any responsibility for issues in a relationship. Remarkably, it's not that people don't want to be responsible. It's more often the case that people don't see their own blind spots, triggers, and underlying cause for the reason they respond to situations the way they do. For example, if you are a man and you grew up knowing your father was cheating on your mother, yet you find infidelity acceptable and you can't see the underlying cause of the problem, you can't see your own blind spot. Dishonor to women in general AND dishonor of your mother was normalized in your household. This is conditioning you aren't even aware of. We are all susceptible to conditioning.

During the time I'm writing this version of this guidebook, it's becoming normalized for people in political office to have "twitter wars" with celebrities and debate policy with late night talk show hosts. The behavior, regardless of political affiliation, is normalizing a certain behavior in offices that represent our nation in the world and we're becoming conditioned to believe that it's okay. It's not okay. We need to set a standard of values, morals, ethics and character in our families. Let's look at an example where someone looks for high morals and character when developing standards for their "family."

Conditioning and normalization happen in our lives, whether we are aware or not. What we have to learn from books like this one and others is that we can control what we take in, what we believe is right for us, and what we expose our families to. Mike Krzyzewski, coach of the five-time National Champions Duke Blue Devils uses the idea of home life conditioning to select his basketball players. Coach K has been tasked to try to find the best talent, but he also tries to find talent that came from two parent homes. Looking deeper into Coach K's thought process, it is worth noting that Duke had very little trouble with kids outside of the classroom and basketball court from 1986 to the present. Coach K was looking for kids who have had the "advantage" of living with their parents, learning lessons from two parents and being more prepared for college life than other students. Some might say he was looking for kids with privilege. I disagree. Coach K looks for kids where parents set the standard. We need to make our African American families, two parent, Christian homes where both parents are wholeheartedly involved **the standard**. I'm stating that what a misguided person might call "privilege" is actually your responsibility to your family.

I share this information to communicate that this is what we want to strive for. We want to have healthy families, which still have struggles, but they work through them together and grow together as a family. The only way to do this is to heal. We have to be committed to healing individually and we need the support of our mate to do this. Everyone has to be involved in the process of healing, but generally the work of healing is up to the individual. Enroll in a group. Take a class. Set up sessions with a therapist. Set up sessions with a coach. Everyone needs to look for context clues to find the areas they need to address. Then be willing to put in the work. Let's figure out how to find the areas to address to begin the healing.

It's important to note here that we must look for what's broken. A few weeks or months after you complete this course, you will be married. Even before that point, you will have spent countless hours with each other. You're not a therapist, counselor or coach, but be aware of things that trigger you or your mate. Be honest with yourself and each other. For example, if you notice something your spouse says often makes you angry, stop and talk about it with your spouse. Could it be that a parent or someone in a past relationship said this in a similar way and reliving that experience triggered you?

A great way to be honest about your internal mental and psychological condition is to have a routine checkup with your spouse. This takes honesty, transparency and most of all, trust on both sides. Ask your spouse periodically, "Babe, what are you seeing in my words or behavior that concerns you?" Don't put conditions on the question or preface it. This is an open-ended question that can lead to a real conversation about any number of things. Ask the question in a comfortable space, where there has been no arguing, fighting or any room for pre-conceived notions. After you have the discussion the first time, then you can explain, you're making sure that your spouse isn't seeing any triggers or anything outside of normal, loving, productive behavior. When you ask the next time, your spouse will understand the context, but the more your relationship develops and strengthens and you continue asking periodically, the better this question will equip each of you to begin healing. If there is a problem in your past causing triggers or other negative or unproductive actions, be honest about it and reach out to a therapist. If a concern is arising about your being blocked or stifled in moving forward and it's not etched in a past trauma or situation, reach out to a coach. They can help you start where you are and move forward in enlightening and productive ways. I would encourage each spouse to ask the other these questions periodically. Preventative maintenance is worth its weight in gold when it comes to our health and well-being.

One of the best ways to heal is to talk through things together and be supportive of each other. Being supportive is instrumental in helping your partner heal. It takes a lot of faith and trust in your mate's integrity to keep these kinds of conversations confidential. If you are the listener, understand the value and belief your partner is putting in you to share this kind of information with you. You matter so much to your mate that you get the opportunity to help them grow. That's huge! Don't let the vulnerability they share with you go unnoticed.

Let's try an exercise. This is a one-on-one exercise with you and your mate only—not a group exercise.

EXERCISE   DATE:

LET'S SHARE

Take ten minutes and tell your mate something that bothered you when you were growing up. It could be something that didn't sit well with you. It can be a lack of trust in a family member, friend, stranger, or parent. It could be major to you or small to you. Whatever it is you share, try to think of something you haven't shared before. This will require a little thought on your part—and a lot of trust—to be vulnerable. You're about to live your lives together forever, being vulnerable is going to become a part of the journey, on both sides. After you share, your partner listens (not a counseling session, just a listening session), let's flip it and have the other partner share the same misuse, abuse, lack of trust or disdain with you. Same process, just listen.

70

EXERCISE

When you finish, I want you to write answers to four questions:

1. Do you feel like your mate heard your story? You shared, but did they listen?

2. Do you feel like your mate was empathetic?

3. How did your mate feel when they heard your story? Describe their feelings.

4. Did you learn something about your mate that you didn't know previously?

After this exercise, I'm guessing you think you are a shade tree, "Dr. Phil," and ready to do some counseling sessions on prime-time TV. I'm joking of course, but I wanted you to do this exercise to see, hear and feel the information that your mate shared. When we listen for understanding, we can help the healing process. Let's be clear, I'm not encouraging anyone to be therapists, coaches, or counselors.

What I am encouraging is that we talk about our problems with the one we love the most. The love of our life takes the time and loves us enough to listen, empathize, and look at how this makes their mate feel and, hopefully, encourages them to take the next step toward healing. You may amaze yourself in how much you and your mate can work through issues together. There could be issues you can't work through together and through conversation you can identify an issue needs work at a professional level. When you look at the symptoms, you can recognize pain. You don't have to be a doctor to know that your finger is broken. You only need to be a doctor to recognize it's a hairline fracture of the fourth metacarpal bone.

Put in the work to keep a psychological health check up on you and your mate. We have to make an extra effort to do this in the black community, as we don't put in the work at the same rate of others. According to the U.S. Department of Health and Human Services Office of Minority Health, adult black/African Americans are *20 percent more likely to report serious psychological distress than adult whites. Despite this, African Americans are less likely than whites to seek out treatment and more likely to end treatment prematurely.* Pro and college athletes have sports psychologists that work with them to help with their careers; CEO's have coaches and therapists that help them work on maintaining their psychological health to manage large companies. Successful marriages require work, too.

Speaking from a perspective of working with many clients and my own personal testimony, put in the work with your loved one, with a coach, counselor, therapist, or pastor. Your spouse is going to support you and, more importantly, it is going to lift a huge weight off of your shoulders and impact your life.

Let's try one more exercise on healing. This can be a group exercise.

PUT IN THE WORK

Everyone in the room has two paper clips. I want you to take one paper clip and straighten it out as perfectly as you can make it. I know there are some perfectionists out there looking for a hammer and flat surface—Lol! It doesn't have to be that straight. Do the best you can with your fingers. Take about two minutes to do this now.

Now, take the second paper clip and simply look at it. Analyze it. Look at the design, where it is straight, where it bends, how many bends, etc. Here is your challenge, should you choose to accept it: Take the straightened paper clip and try to put it back to its exact original shape— just like the example paper clip. Take about two minutes to work on your project.

Put your paperclip, your mate's paper clip and your original paper clips on a table or piece of paper in front of you. What do you see? I'm going to take a wild guess and say that no one was able to get the paper clip back to its original form. You even had another example of the desired result (the second paper clip) to look at while you did your master craftsmanship!

The point of this exercise is for each of you to understand this: We can see the imperfections in ourselves, in each other and in our marriages. We can see how those imperfections came to be and how they unfolded in our lives. Now, we want to get it back to where it was or even better, we want to be better than we ever have been! This is a great goal. The truth of the matter is, we need to find the imperfections, do what we can do to begin the healing, then seek professional assistance to make the paper clip as close to perfect as possible, while remembering that it will never be exactly the same.

Once you have changed the original shape of the paper clip, try to use it. It may work a little, but you'll find that it probably won't hold papers the same way it did before. Similarly, your imperfections can come back or sometimes become exaggerated. Your paper clip needs maintenance (some extra bending, maybe heating with a lighter), so that assistance you received as professional help to work toward your healing, should continue as maintenance.

Ignore stigmas with your friends, family or anyone else who doesn't understand or doesn't like the fact that you do what you have to for your healing. There is no shame of going to any doctor, just as there is no shame to go to anyone who offers psychological, marital, or mental health support. The only shame related to healing support inside or outside of the marriage, would be the fact that it's a shame you didn't do everything possible to receive the healing you deserve to be the best husband or wife for your spouse.

Chapter Nine

You don't do that thing you used to do...

Understanding sex in marriage. It's not taboo; quite the opposite.

Ooooh. I bet some ears perked up when they read the title. Talking about premarital sex? In the church? Don't try to leave...sit right on back down! Lol! I can see people grabbing purses and hats as I type. Yep, we're going to go there...but not quite yet.

There is a lot to share in this chapter, but one of the most important points is this: sex is not taboo. This is a misnomer. Sex is a blessing from God, designed to enhance marriage. Sex is more than the vehicle for procreation, intercourse with your spouse is a beautiful reflection of your intimacy with each other. 1 Corinthians 7:5 is often quoted in sermons and biblical lessons because it talks about not depriving one another from sex other than by mutual consent for a time so that you may devote yourselves in prayer. We often hear that we should not deprive each other of sex in marriage and I agree. The point must be made at the end of the passage that says, "then come together again so that the Satan will not tempt you because of lack of self-control." That's how important our sex lives are in the marriage journey. We need to remain intimate not only to satisfy our spouse (which should be our number one priority), but we need to be together to truly fight the temptation of the world. People commit adultery for a plethora of reasons. I'm not saying that sex or lack thereof is the only reason for adultery. What I want you to consider is we can take sex off of the table as a reason for adultery if we manage our sex lives with the intent of pleasing our spouse.

My Pledge

A couple of my friends in the helping professions (coaching, counselors, therapists, etc.) have made this comment to me: "We're always working to get married people in the bed and single people out of it." Having sex when you're single does a lot of things (that I won't touch on in this guidebook), but there's one thing it doesn't do at all: Single sex is a poor representation of sex inside of marriage. I don't want that to sound disappointing or discouraging. Quite the opposite. Let's keep it 100: single sex is sex with no commitment or at best a pseudo-commitment. Here are three thoughts that people don't generally say out loud, but definitely cross their minds during sexual relationships when single:

"I'll be down for you as long as I can't find a better option."

"As long as you keep doing that thing you do, and I don't have a more significant requirement than what this looks like, we're good."

"This works for me, why complicate it with marriage? If I'm required to actually pay for the cow, I can go find some other free milk somewhere else."

These thoughts confirm one important reality: Single sex requires the minimum commitment. Married sex is the exact opposite. It is the definition of commitment. I'm giving you my body, unconditionally. It's not available to anyone else. My body is designed to serve my spouse sexually, from this day forward. My pledge to you is that I'm yours, whether we're upset with each other, not feeling each other, in a different country, on a different continent, we don't have any money, your body has changed, the kids are acting out or our family is going through a rough patch. None of that matters. I. AM. YOURS. In the words of the great philosopher, T.I., "point blank, period."

It should be a focus of you and your mate to both be engaged and contribute to your sex life. We're still talking commitment here. When you first get married, you won't have a problem engaging or committing. This is the day you have been waiting for! You can get as much as you want and Heaven approves! There's nothing like it. It's great and it should be. You deserve to communicate your love verbally, emotionally, psychologically, and physically. There will be a time when everything isn't what it used to be.

Marriage is work. Sex is work. Yes, literally, but I'm saying that sex is more than fun and more than a duty to your spouse. It's a required commitment to your marriage. Husbands, having sex with your wives is another way of saying, "I love you, I want you, and I'm committed." Wives, having sex with your Husbands is a way of saying "I appreciate you, I respect you and what you do for your family, and I want to please you." That engagement, that focused energy, is important. Put it on the calendar if need be. Whatever you can come up with to make sure both of you stay engaged and focused to get it in, when it's not convenient or even when you two aren't at the best place in your marriage.

Sex brings closeness. Sex reiterates our intimacy. Especially in our community, sex reinforces we have each other's back when the world is throwing shade at us, at work, school, in the community, wherever the challenge may be. Sex also reflects a divine connection between husband and wife. Ephesians 5:31 reads "The two will become one flesh." There is a connection between a husband and wife that is strengthened spiritually in their sex lives. Sex in marriage is a direct reflection of your connection and your connection is a direct reflection of your sex life. The two are inseparable—as it should be.

Not Going Back. We're Moving Forward

When we start a new marriage, we have to understand we are starting something brand new. Whatever the context of our relationship was the day before we married changed on the day we said "I do." Israel Houghton has a beautiful song that says, "I'm not going back, I'm moving ahead, I'm here to declare to you, the past is over." The song is called "Moving Forward" and Israel is saying that he's not going back to his old life. He is surrendering his life to Christ. We want you to understand there is a surrender to move forward in your new marriage. Surrender your single life, surrender your ego, surrender your self-preservation, and surrender your sex life. When you do this, you can move forward.

I'm Not Going Back

This means in your sex life, you can't go back. You can't make comparisons to premarital sex, whether it was with your spouse or someone else. You cannot have expectations based on what happened before. This is where the devil shows up in our sex lives. He wants you to compare your spouse to someone else. He wants you to compare what you did before with whomever to what you do now in covenant. The enemy wants you to look back and think that things could have been better based on a sexual encounter that happened with someone that had no commitment or interest in your well-being.

Can I tell you something? You can't base your current expectations on previous situations. You have to be ok with understanding mentally and psychologically: I'm not going back. When the Bible says that premarital sex wasn't good for us, it wasn't to indict us to be penalized for something we couldn't adhere to. God knew the end from the beginning. The enemy uses our past sex lives to interfere with the best, most incredible bond of all—sex inside of marriage. The grass is not greener on the other side. You have AstroTurf over in your house—it doesn't get any greener than that, but you have to maintain it! When you make the conscious decision that sexually you're not going back, now you can take the next step.

I'm Moving Ahead

We have decided we aren't going back. The next step is to move ahead. Moving forward means to progress. Moving forward means we have left the old stuff behind. There is no condemnation in our new lives. Whatever we did before is no longer. We have made a spiritual, lifetime commitment. It's time to move forward in our sex life as well. This means you can want and have your spouse as much as you agree to it. There is no condemnation in the marital bed. The key here is to recognize it's on you to maintain this new sexual journey together. It is up to each of you to keep the spice in your sex life and not be ashamed of whatever it is you two desire. It's on you, just for you!

As scripture says, the marriage bed is undefiled. Undefiled has several meanings, but the one I want to point out is "without blemish." What you do in your bed with your spouse is without blemish. It is incorruptible. I want to point this out for those who have saved themselves for marriage. You did what God wanted you to do. Now, you get to enjoy all of the benefits of waiting. Again, don't think its taboo. Society would have us believe either extreme, sex is fine with whomever, wherever, whenever or the opposite, sex is bad and only for procreation. Both commentaries couldn't be further from the truth. If you have waited, God sees your purity, but He expects you to enjoy what he has for you in marriage. Please your spouse, serve your spouse and enjoy your spouse, sexually. Decide to move forward in this way.

I'm Here to Declare, the Past is Over

The reality in the black community is there is quite a bit of insecurity in many facets of our lives. It may or may not be sexually related, but this insecurity can influence our sex lives. How one spouse feels about another's past relationship and exploits can affect a marriage and by default, your sex life. There are those of us who are dealing with insecurity in our marriage, whether perceived or real. I want you to assure and reassure your spouse, by declaring the past is over. When you get into this thing called marriage and you're sleeping in the same bed wanting to do things you may not have done before, some of us are going to naturally think about the past. Some people are going to be distracted because they "knew" you before you were married. They knew what you did with other people. They knew what you were capable of. I'm sure some of you are reading this and wondering "how does this have anything to do with sex?" It has everything to do with sex. There needs to be a new, undeniable trust between two people to share their bodies with each other. There are cases where you will need to be ready, willing and able to declare the past is the past, we're moving forward together and there is no one else. The truth of the matter is trust is built over time through a sequence of showing one's self trustworthy. The more you show yourself trustworthy, the more you will be trusted. Husbands, if a woman is trusting you with her body, her curves, her imperfections and all of her nuances, you must be able to show her your love for her is unconditional. Sex for a woman is an emotional connection with spiritual overtones. You must be willing to be vulnerable for her as well as showing her she can trust you with all of the vulnerability sex in marriage brings. The past is over. Sacrifice your past so that you can move forward, sexually and otherwise, together.

EXERCISE

DATE: _____

THE PAST IS OVER

The couple that gives the best story about how they have decided to move forward in their marriage because of a sexually-related topic will win a prize.

Chapter Ten

A Successful Marriage is a Threesome

Covenant is a bond between husband, wife, and God

The word, "marriage" is used too loosely in today's society. We use the word marriage sometimes to make a statement of commitment (or no commitment), i.e. "I'm not married to the idea of adding another employee." "I'm married to my work," etc. Marriage should stand alone in its explanation of an earthly connection between a man and a woman sanctified by God and witnessed before others. I just made marriage sound like a big deal, right? It is a big deal! It's a very big deal! We don't have to take ourselves and our relationships seriously all of the time, but we often take marriage and sometimes our own marriages too lightly. This is real. Marriage is the biggest commitment you will ever make with one exception—accepting Christ as your savior. You are going through pre-marriage counseling, but what you are really experiencing is a cleansing, healing and awareness that you are about to have the most intense relationship you will ever experience. Covenant.

Covenant is defined by Merriam-Webster as a "formal, solemn, and binding agreement." Now, let's take that up a notch. Marital Covenant is a formal, solemn, and binding agreement between you, your spouse, and God. You agree to have each other though better or worse, in sickness and health, for richer or poorer as long as you both shall live. The hidden emphasis is you two agree, understanding and making a vow to God to be there for your spouse for as long as you live. I'm not going to bore you with too many definitions, but I believe another definition is important here. You are making a vow. Merriam-Webster says a vow is: "A solemn promise or assertion, specifically, one by which a person is bound to an act, service or condition." This tells us that a vow is your unconditional promise to serve your spouse, and you made the promise to God, to your spouse and in the witness of those you honor and value. This is how we express covenant.

Covenant in Scripture

The word covenant in scripture is often used as God's promise to man. Exodus 34:10 says, "Then the Lord said: 'I am making a covenant with you. Before all your people I will do wonders never before done in any nation in all the world. The people you live among will see how awesome is the work that I, the Lord, will do for you.'" The Lord made a promise—a holy promise—to Moses to let him know he would protect the Israelites on their journey from Egypt, and He did just that. There are 332 examples of covenant in one form or another in the Bible. Although the context slightly differs in each example, the premise is the same throughout the text: A holy promise between God and His people or Christ and His people. It's important to understand this promise is not a normal promise. People break promises as frequently as drivers change lanes. It happens every day, all day. Some broken promises are intentional, some are not. That said, it's important to understand going into marriage, especially in our community where we have experienced broken promises from society more than other cultures (40 acres and a mule, desegregated schools, equality through affirmative action, etc.), this promise is not like any other promise on earth. This promise is not of earth. This is a spiritually-based promise that you're going to rock with your spouse through all of it. The ebbs and flows of life. Ups and downs. Financially independent or robbing Peter to pay Paul. This promise says you have her back and she has yours (men) forever and ever, amen.

Covenant is bigger than you understand. Let me put it this way, people can pervert the word or the idea of the institution of marriage for their own pleasure or agenda, but it doesn't matter. The covenant you develop when you take each other's hand in marriage is a commitment that fulfills the promise of God. Matthew 19:4 reads "'Haven't you read," he replied, 'that at the beginning the Creator 'made them male and female, and said, 'For this reason a man will leave his father and mother and be united to his wife, and the two will become one flesh'? So they are no longer two, but one flesh. Therefore, what God has joined together, let no one separate." You have read this scripture at some point, but have you really thought about it? Marriage is so serious Christ Himself said a man is leaving his father and mother. Your parents are your foundation. They made you and raised you. They poured into you. But today, my son, you are out! You have been told by the Most High, it's time to move on. That's deep when you really think about it.

Mama's boys, like the ones that put their mom before their wife, need not apply. This is not the job for you. Step up and put your wife first. Period. Next, the scripture says let what God has joined together let no one separate. Essentially, this marriage—this union right here—this is permanent! I put the exclamation point so you could see it in print. There is no out. Divorce is not an option. Matthew 19:8: "Jesus replied, 'Moses permitted you to divorce your wives because your hearts were hard. But it was not this way from the beginning.'" Let's dig into this a bit.

Not Optional

I mentioned this before, but it's worth repeating: My awesome wife told me before we were married that divorce is off the table. It's not optional. It's not up for consideration. There will be no vote, no conversation, no discussion, no deliberation, no review, no debate. Divorce is not an option.

Think about this scripture. This is this epitome of the covenant of marriage. Malachi 2:16 "The man who hates and divorces his wife," says the Lord, the God of Israel, "does violence to the one he should protect," says the Lord Almighty. Divorce is not only separation, but it does violence to the woman he should protect. Men, your commitment to protect her in every way removes divorce as an option.

At this point, you are over half-way through this program. I'm going to encourage you to marinate and think on what you learn about removing divorce as an option. This is a transitional period in how you think about your spouse. Starting today, I want you to agree that divorce is not an option. This is a huge commitment, but this is an important part of the foundation of your marriage. Not this book, not the ring on your hand and not even the butterflies as you walk down the aisle—none of that is the foundation. The promise is the foundation, but this commitment that divorce is off the table is the cornerstone of the foundation of the marriage.

Christ said, it was not this way from the beginning. God never meant for divorce to be an option. He covers you in ways you can't even fathom when you join together in covenant with Him. Why would you break that covenant?

Some people will look for outs. She doesn't manage money well, he cheated, etc. You're not committed if you're looking for outs. If you're looking for a backup plan, you want to leave this class and go to the backup plan now. Marriage to the person next to you isn't for you.

Alternatives

Anyone who has spent some time in corporate America knows that when you come to your boss with a problem, they really want to hear that you have already devised a solution. Marriage is no different. I'm a coach and people come to me with why they want to leave a marriage often. Rarely is it the case that people come to me with a problem and even the beginning of a solution. I understand that people don't have the tools to solve the problem many times, but what you must have is the heart to desire a solution. Marriage isn't easy, but marriage is like any institution, it's a work in progress. Always work together on alternatives to overcome situations. Life will lead you to believe there is only one answer and there is no alternative. Work together in the challenges of your marriage. Think outside of the box. I know you will find multiple alternatives that lead to solutions if you talk through things together.

EXERCISE

DATE:

The Trifecta

If my title of this chapter was online, some people would consider it click-bait, because some would say it insinuates one thing when it really talks about another. That idea can be left to perspective, but the truth is successful marriage requires a threesome. Each of you must stay connected to your faith. Each of you must stay connected to the Word. Each of your must have a personal, intimate relationship with God. There will be times when only that personal relationship with God will carry you through. He is in your relationship. He's all up in it. He's in your finances. He's in your sex life. He's in your careers. He's in your parenting. He's in your relationship with your in-laws. He's in your dreams and desires. He's in your prayers. He's in you. You must allow God to inhabit you.

When Steph Curry shoots and makes (that was redundant—if Steph shoots—he makes!) a three pointer, he puts up three fingers. I think we need to do that in marriage. When you celebrate a new job, a move to another city or get a good report from the doctor, put up the "Three." When you do something that impacts your community, your world, your house, or your closet, because the closet was just looking a mess, put up the "Three." God is in all of this, fam. He's the architect of the awesomeness of your marriage. God completes the trifecta in marriage. Recognize this and honor Him.

EXERCISE

DATE:

TRIFECTA

Let's have some fun with the Three. I want every couple to develop their own handshake (at home) and incorporate the three. Three fingers, three hands, three toes... whatever. When we come to class next time, each couple is going to show off their handshake with the Three involved. I encourage you to continue doing the handshake from time to time after marriage. Revise it. Change it. Do whatever you like. Have fun with it. Do me a favor... keep the Three in it. Let's recognize the reason your marriage is so incredible!

Before we move on, I want to mention one other sports reference about the Trifecta. Matt Stover was a kicker for the Baltimore Ravens in the NFL. Matt did something you don't see with other kickers. You often see kickers "point to heaven" after they make a kick. Players often pray or "point to heaven" after they score a touchdown. Stover also pointed when he missed a kick. He was acknowledging that God was the most important thing in his life whether the kick went through the uprights or not.

We must do the same thing. When things don't work out how we want them to, we must acknowledge him. Point to Him (proverbially) when things are their worst. When your marriage sucks. When you lose someone you love. When you can't get pregnant. When you have more kids than you can afford. Point. To. Him. Whatever the challenge, the trifecta doesn't change. It doesn't matter how much good you do, or how much bad you do. Matthew 5:45 says, "that you may be children of your Father in heaven. He causes his sun to rise on the evil and the good and sends rain on the righteous and the unrighteous." Trouble is coming. You don't have to look for it. I promise, it's coming. Also understand, trouble doesn't last always. Whether it's good or bad that you are in at the moment, or whatever you two experience tomorrow, continue to point to him.

Chapter Eleven

I was Raised Baptist

Understanding the importance of being on the same page in decisions on faith and worship

Just for the record, I wasn't raised Baptist, but I wanted to get my point across. When the two become one flesh, we often still have two denominations with different doctrines, different traditions, different expectations and sometimes even different theologies. This is an important conversation that sometimes gets overlooked because "he can provide for my child" or "she can cook like my mama." "We'll figure it out after we're married," is not an acceptable answer to decisions on how to move forward on in worship. Remember, we just talked about God being the center of the trifecta, but how you worship God impacts your expression of how you see Him in your relationship. Families need to be on the same page with how they choose to worship.

One Size Does Not Fit All

I once knew a couple that worshiped at different churches. The wife attended my church and the husband attended another church. Regardless of that difference, they were unified in their faith. So much so, that the husband would take trips and do things with our church that he didn't do with his own church. They had the kind of relationship where this arrangement not only worked for them, they thrived in it. Let me keep it 100 with you again; that wouldn't work for me. I need my wife next to me when I'm praising. I need to agree in faith, worship and in presence when we worship. There are exceptions (traveling separately, etc.), but in general, we pray together, worship together and stay together. It works for us. Let's be clear, it's no better or worse than the first example in this section. Both couples are filled. Both couples are fed. Both couples praise our Lord and both couples are unified about how it is done. There is no one size fits all in how you decide to worship.

Win-Win

What you must consider is to come up with a solution that works for both of you. If one person is not happy in this decision, it doesn't work. Compromise is an unacceptable solution here. This has to be a win-win situation. Whatever it takes, regardless of time, both people must be happy (not ok) with the decision. We deserve to worship in a space where our needs are met. It may be a change from what we are used to, but we need to have a space where we can serve, and worship where we are comfortable. This reiterates that one size doesn't fit all. We have to agree on what fits us. Spend time working through whether or not the substance fits what you require. Style matters to some as well. You have to feel comfortable receiving the message and you must feel comfortable sharing your lives with the church. Work on this until you both come up with a win-win for everyone. You will be happy you put in the work.

The Body Supersedes Doctrine (in Marriage)

I don't know if I have said something controversial to this point, but I'm about to: Being a part of the body of Christ is far more important than doctrinal beliefs. I will explain, but allow me to expound a bit. Every denomination has its own set of traditions, beliefs, and doctrine. The Pew Research Center states that in Atlanta, GA alone, there are currently 121 Christian denominations (including non-denominational churches). I'm sure they could pare it down even farther, but my point is, even within a denomination, there are doctrinal differences. I'm not minimizing the importance of doctrine within a church, but I'm definitely minimizing the importance of doctrine within a marriage. If you have decided to take this journey together, the two of you must have this conversation now. What does worship together look like? Let me share three things you should consider when you're considering the worship you want to be a part of. If this is a Christian marriage, these three components should be a part of your worship together.

1. Christ is our Savior. If you're Muslim, as is the case with some of my Muslim friends, you don't agree. If you are a non-Messianic Jew, you don't agree. That's fine, it's not a debatable point. This is the cornerstone of all Christian faith.

2. Christ died and rose again. It's kind of the main point. Christ was sent to pay for our sins. Again, some of my brothers and sisters who align with other faiths disagree. It's important for you to understand, if you are a Christian, His death and resurrection is essential to our salvation. It's our only option.

3. Christ was a servant leader. While Jesus was on earth, He served. He served in multiple capacities. He fed the multitudes who listened to Him speak. He turned water into wine. He gave the blind man sight, restored the ear of the Roman soldier and gave life to Lazarus. Jesus washed the feet of His disciples. When you really look into scripture, Christ taught, but He also served. He wants us to serve. Praise Him. Worship Him. Serve others.

EXERCISE

DATE:

TRADITIONS

When we come from different backgrounds, we learn different things, we express our worship through different traditions. Write down three traditions you have experienced in your faith and worship growing up. Share them with your mate. You may learn something about them you didn't know before. This exercise is not to judge what is good or bad, right or wrong or acceptable vs unacceptable. This exercise is to learn about your mate's upbringing with no judgement. Talk about these traditions for five minutes per person. What do you remember about them? Are they important to you? Talk about what makes them important.

Equally Yoked

In his second letter to the Corinthians, Paul was clear about being with unbelievers. 2 Corinthians 6:14 says, "Do not be yoked together with unbelievers. For what do righteousness and wickedness have in common?" Ouch! He made it plain, though. The point that Paul is really trying to make is expressed later in the chapter. 6:16 says: "For we are the temple of the living God. As God has said: 'I will live with them and walk among them, and I will be their God, and they will be my people.'" God is communicating that He wants to dwell with people who look to Him as their God and follows His word.

Being unequally yoked produces unimaginable challenges when we think about it. Are we celebrating the same holidays? Do we celebrate holidays at all? Where do we worship? Where do our children worship? How do we respect each other's worship? What if something I'm doing directly conflicts with your worship—how do we resolve? I have seen people who are unequally yoked. When determined enough, people can make just about anything work. Making it work is not thriving. If I'm playing basketball with one hand behind my back and my shoes tied together, I'm not starting off on an even playing field when we start the game. I have decisive disadvantages. This is what happens when we are unequally yoked. Most of the time, the domineering personality wins. This creates resentment. The attitude permeates in everything the couple does. We want to start any relationship, any marriage with the ability to be happy and successful.

Paul discusses the fact that a woman married to an unbeliever sanctifies the husband and a man married to an unbeliever sanctifies the wife. It is so. That said, let's not make life harder than it has to be. A believer knowingly marrying an unbeliever is unequally yoked. I know people in this circumstance. It sucks. Imagine what it's like for one person to have to keep their relationship with God in secret instead of expressing it and enjoying it with their spouse. If your spouse has a change of heart in the marriage, you committed to stay and you should definitely stay in the marriage. The enemy comes to steal, kill and destroy and this is an example of the enemy walking into your marriage. Prepare for spiritual battle in that instance. For the purposes of where you are right now and where you are headed, don't walk into the enemy's lair. Someone who doesn't believe isn't ready for what you have to offer. If you really love them, allow them the time and space to come to learn about the love of Christ.

If you want joy in your life and you want them to have joy, understand that this is not the way to connect with them. Nothing replaces the spiritual connection of a wife and a husband. If one is not connected, there is no trifecta. You can't even do the handshake and throw up the 3! Let them grow in Christ on their own. Share the message with them, but let them walk it out and allow God to give you what is best for you—someone who is equally yoked.

EXERCISE

DATE: _____

EQUALLY YOKED

What was the most fun thing you did in church growing up? Think back to what you did and share this experience with your spouse. What was did you like about it? Was there something that happened specifically that makes you remember this experience. Spend 5 minutes each sharing your experience.

Chapter Twelve

Riding a Tandem Bike Versus Playing Tug of War

Coordinating a vision to guide the direction of the marriage.

Have you ever seen anyone ride a tandem bike in person? If you google "riding a tandem bike" the first thing that comes up as of this publishing is: "Riding a tandem requires teamwork, though. The front rider (captain) does all the steering and braking, which means earning and keeping the trust of the rear rider (stoker). For most tandem bikes, the riders must pedal in sync at the same rate, which means compromise."

If you ever have the chance, try to ride a tandem bike, preferably with your spouse. It takes coordination between the captain and the stoker. The second person on the bike has to pedal in synch with the captain. They can't pedal faster or slower. They can't decide to coast if the captain isn't coasting. They have to start on the same foot and pedal at the same rate. The opening quote says the riders compromise, but I think better stated is the riders cooperate. They are working together for the greater good. The second rider may be the better rider and may have a different plan for where they want to go, but they can't. They have to follow the vision of the captain, because the captain decides the direction (vision), they can shift direction or stop completely. If they are riding well, the captain alerts the stoker of a stop and they stop pedaling simultaneously.

We have all played Tug of War at some point in school. It is just as the title says…we're tugging to win the war. We work in unison with our team, but it quickly becomes apparent the strengths and weaknesses of both teams. The interesting thing is most of the times I have played Tug of War, I have found that everyone doesn't pull together with the same energy at the same time. Someone has to win, so ultimately, the team that does the best job of pulling together with the same energy at the same time and balancing strengths and weaknesses wins. In a game of *mano y mano* (hand to hand combat), this can work, but in life trying to time when to pull together and hide weaknesses, it is generally a losing proposition.

Choosing the Path

Relationships require some form of leadership. If no one leads, no one goes anywhere. Leadership doesn't equate to being someone's boss or someone's master. Leadership is really about building a relationship with those you lead, building trust with those you lead, communication with those you lead and personal accountability of the leader. Notice, I didn't say being bossy or making it happen. Nope. Leading is finding direction with people who believe in you and agreeing to move in the suggested direction. It goes back to the tandem bike. Leading on a tandem bike requires trust. Leading in tug of war requires force. The tandem bike managed properly will always arrive at its destination. A team in a tug of war is limited by the amount of force it can muster at a given time. It can work from time to time, but playing tug of war, is not a good strategy to achieving goals. Leadership in marriage first requires the leader to choose a path, with the counsel of the rest of the team. Let's take a look at who leads and why.

Loving Your Wife

Ephesians 5:21-24 says, "Submit to one another out of reverence for Christ. Wives, submit yourselves to your own husbands as you do to the

Lord. For the husband is the head of the wife as Christ is the head of the church, his body, of which he is the Savior. Now as the church submits to Christ, so also wives should submit to their husbands in everything." If you're in this class, you have read this before. We see that we are called for the husband to lead the marriage. The challenge in marriages, especially in the black community is what does that really look like? Throughout the sessions I have experienced and many people I have discussed this topic with, I believe the challenge is addressed in verse 21. Submit to one another...out of reverence...for Christ. Let's look at each of the three parts of the verse.

Submitting to One Another

When you lead as I mentioned earlier 1. In relationship, 2. With trust, 3. Communicating and 4. Taking personal responsibility and accountability, as a leader, you are submitting to your wife. Your "submission" has shown you put her needs first and you take responsibility for her protection and safety in the marriage. When Christ was leading his disciples a little over 2,000 years ago, he was submitting to people, when he didn't have to do it. He didn't have to go to the house to save the little girl who was sick. He didn't have to save the blind man or raise Lazarus from the dead. He made a choice, although He was already the King of Kings and Lord of Lords to submit to the needs of His people. Keep something in mind: Christ submitted first. He submitted by those works in the Bible, but most importantly, He submitted to His Father's will for us by dying on the cross. He is our example of submission. Husbands, submit to your wives first.

Out of Reverence

This means a feeling of deep respecting tinged with awe. Let that sink in. We submit to one another because of the respect and awe we have for Jesus. Ladies, the reverence that you have for Christ is shown in the respect you give to your husband when you submit to him. I know you love him. I also know that in year 3, he will do something that gets on your nerves. He says he's leading, but you don't see the fruit of it. You would rather throw some fruit at him! You submit to him, you honor your husband and follow his vision out of reverence—

not for him, but for Christ. Remember, this man loves you and wants the best for you. He's committed and he's leading. He's also quite imperfect and flawed. He trusts you, communicates with you and honors you. He should be showing you committed leadership, which is indeed submission to you. Wives, honor your Savior by submitting to your husband. Out of reverence.

For Christ

This sounds pretty self-explanatory, right? Eh, I don't think so. When we get down to it, we should do everything because 'God so loved the world that He gave his only begotten son, and whosoever believes in Him should not perish, but have ever-lasting life.' (John 3:16). The reality is, we work toward that goal, but life happens and we don't always achieve the mark. We should continue to work toward this calling, but I want you to know marriage ups the ante. For Christ. He blessed your marriage, before you were a twinkle in your daddy's eye. He said it. Paul wrote it. Christ didn't bless your car in the Bible. He wasn't speaking life over your Mercedes. He didn't promise you the new six-figure career. Nope. That makes this even more powerful! Paul took the time to say submit to one another out of reverence for Christ. This means your reverence to Christ is the "door opening" for Jesus to bless your marriage. You're going to need it. You don't know it today but ask your leaders. Ask them if their marriages have needed blessings they couldn't have even imagined before they got married. Ephesians 5:33 reads, "Each one of you also must love his wife as he loves himself, and the wife must respect her husband." For Christ. Love her like no one else. For Christ. Respect him to the utmost. For Christ. When you put "for Christ" on the end of the concept, it makes it real and most importantly, it makes it undeniable.

Setting the Table and Executing

When we go to the office for work, whether we work for a company of 10 or a company of 100,000, someone is setting the vision. Whenever we attend a committee meeting or a PTA meeting, someone is setting a vision for the coming year and things we would like to accomplish. If we're playing spades and calling books, someone is setting the vision (and if you're on my team and you set it wrong, we're going to have a problem – Lol!). With every organized activity in life, someone is setting the vision. Marriage is no different. As I said before, take the premise of riding a tandem bike. Set your direction (vision) then execute (pedal, steer and brake when necessary, together). Let's expound on execution.

When you work together to set the vision of different components of marriage, understand that it is said "without vision, the people perish," but without execution to the vision, you won't get where you're trying to go. Let's point the finger for a moment...not at you...at the author. I'm great at casting vision. Let's go! Let's have a pep rally and get this thing started. I have ideas for days and there are so many in my head I can't communicate them all. Now, execution, that's a different story. It's not my calling, not my lane (did someone just cop out?..wait there's more). It's true that we must know how to play the role we are gifted to do. That said, it's not an option not to execute, it's a requirement. You have to put in the work, together. Sometimes, you may have to do something uncomfortable. You may have to do something that doesn't fit in your lane. Check this out: it doesn't matter. My friends at Nike put it like this: JUST.DO.IT.

Make room for the gifts and talents you have. If someone is casting the vision, while you have all of these great ideas, also find the right ways to accomplish the mission. Here's an example: If you want to save $10,000 in 2 years, but the man sucks at managing the bank account and the woman is an accountant and is willing and capable to manage the money—it doesn't matter who brings it home—let her execute. Get out of your own way. There is value in traditional roles but find roles that fit your marriage. Don't do something that conflicts with scripture, but don't be apprehensive to do your marriage your way.

I gave this the subtitle of setting the table and executing. This is a pool refence. The table is set up. The great pool player sees the vision of his strategy and executes. Cast the vision. Make it plain. Work on it together. Execute.

EXERCISE

DATE:

CASTING VISION & EXECUTING STRATEGY

Casting Vision, Executing Strategy. This game requires a group. You will get to work together on your vision casting and how to strategize, together! We're going to play the game many of us played as a child—we called it "Concentration." You can play with cards, laying them out on a table and flipping over cards to match a card that was previously flipped. This one will be a little different. There are 16 pictures on the screen (cards flipped over). These cards are not 2 of the exact same cards, they are two cards where one card goes with another (for example, a glove and a ball, a cell phone and a charger, Starbucks logo and coffee, etc.). The team that gets the most matches (taking turns) wins. The team has to decide on strategy, who makes the call, how to make the calls, etc. Every team gets one turn on the first time around. After the first time, if a team gets a match, they get to call two more cards.

Chapter Thirteen

"Crypto" currency
Taking the mystery out of managing finances in marriage

We finally made it. I'm sure a lot of you have been waiting for this chapter. I'm sure some of you are wondering why this chapter isn't first, middle and last in this book. I get it. How we manage financial matters is always different. We're raised different. We see our parents make money stretch enough to take care of several kids and the household. Sometimes, we see our parents struggle with money management skills and that becomes our normal. Some of us manage money meticulously, which quite frankly may get on your mate's nerves. Another important factor of how we develop our concept of money is most of us in the black community aren't taught very much about money as we grow up. We hear things like "go to college, get a good job." The implication is our income will sustain us, but it can't sustain us if we don't know how to manage it.

Here's a point you never hear, but you need to know: Your income is your greatest wealth building asset. We are led to believe our money is designed to go from our bank account to Georgia Power, AT&T and GMAC (General Motors' finance company). That couldn't be further from the truth. We each have specific basic needs in life, but everything else we decide to do is determined by what we prioritize. Essentially, your financial decisions are less a question of being good or bad with money, but moreover exemplary of what you have determined is a priority in your life. Let's work through how to think about prioritizing, how to prioritize together and how to execute to the mission. Most people struggle with executing to the mission, but in actuality they don't know what the mission really is. Diving in...

Pebble Beach

I'm a golfer. Not a very good one, but count me among the many who want to chase the little white ball around a farm disguised as a course, with trucked in sand to make a difficult game even harder; to put said ball in a 4.25-inch hole...18 times...in the fewest shots possible. It's a hobby, passion, sickness...whatever you want to call it. I spend too much money and time playing a game I will likely only get marginally better at over my lifetime—but I love it! The bigger challenge than putting the little ball into the Starbucks cup-sized hole is this game is expensive! Exclamation mark expensive! If you have ever been "ballin' on a budget" like I have, you find ways to play and make it affordable, without a doubt. That said, there are things like green fees that are non-negotiable. If you want to play at a certain course, you have to pay whatever their fee is. This brings me to my challenge with a certain course and my priorities.

Pebble Beach Golf Links. There's a photo on this page. Look at the majestic beauty of the course with the backdrop of the Pacific Ocean. Spectacular! I want to be there. I NEED to be there. I would likely be there right now if I could. Fellow golfers know the challenge before they read this: The green fees! The green fees for Pebble Beach are $525.00 plus a $40 cart fee, plus $92.50 per bag for the caddie—each day. Most packages require you to play the course and its sister course over two days. Of course, I have to have food and drink while I'm there, and I have yet to buy a plane ticket, rent a car or book my hotel. This is an expensive challenge. *We* (my wife and I) must decide how, when and if we should work to overcome it. We have to decide where the priority of playing Pebble Beach falls in our lives.

PAINTING PICTURES

I really wanted to paint the picture of Pebble Beach for you. Now, take your own top three hobbies or desire. Maybe you collect purses, shoes, or sports cars. Think about the thing you want the most. Take about three minutes and describe your version of what this looks like to you. Maybe it's taking a trip to Paris, Hawaii, or Miami. Maybe it's going to the Megafest Conference or visiting where Christ actually walked in Israel. It could be buying a house or getting a degree. It could be moving to Atlanta or LA to pursue music or acting. Whatever that thing is, describe your best version of it to your group. Share that feeling so everyone can appreciate your passion.

Here's a quick footnote to keep in your mind during this chapter: Everyone has a different level of what is "a lot" and what isn't a lot for them. Put simply, $1,000.00 to me may equate to five cents to Mark Cuban. No couple's finances are the same. Everything truly is relative. Don't get caught up in the example, remember it's relative. Focus on the message.

I can book Pebble Beach today, if I so desire. But is it really the priority on our list, or is it something that doesn't fit within our current financial situation? Candidly, if you know me, you know my spiritual gift of faith sometimes shows through. I can get it twisted, though. I could spend the money and say to my wife "God will provide our bills and everything we need." The reality is, that's true. But let's be clear—he already did. I just want to chase that little white ball so much, I'm ready to consider misappropriating some funds! Misappropriation is for corrupt politicians, not husbands that are protecting and providing for their wives.

That was a lot of lead up to the message, but it's important you get what I'm saying here: You and your spouse are in *control* of every penny you earn. Every. Single. Dollar. There's a big difference in the financial mentality in the black community and other cultures. A former manager of mine several years ago told me something I never forgot. He told me he was buying his house through Countrywide Mortgage (long before the housing crisis of 2008). He said it didn't matter what happened to anything he owned. Countrywide could take his house. The auto finance company could take his car. He was ALWAYS going to pay himself FIRST. His intent was to always pay his bills, on time, but his income was his income and he was always going to pay himself first, before any bill. Now, as Christians we are instructed to tithe.

I believe tithing is biblical. I'm going to talk about that later in the chapter. Therefore, let me remix a little of what my manager told me. Tithe first (give God some of what He is giving you). Second, pay yourself. It's amazing what we think we need, but in actuality it's what we are used to or what we want because we prioritize things that aren't necessities. Our lack of proper prioritization reflects a lack of control. We can go even deeper into our environment seeing people who didn't control money and didn't talk about money. We can wallow in the past, but we're getting married, we're moving toward the future. Let's take control. Together. I can hit you over the head with a lot of scriptures, financial gurus, and strategies, but we can walk this out without the stress. It takes being purposeful about your priorities, merging your habits, and being consistent. Let's review strategies and commentary.

What Do You Want, Boo?

What is your priority? We have established I want to play Pebble Beach. In our house, at the time of this release, it's not enough of a priority financially to make it happen. As a matter of fact, doing that selfish act would interfere with some other things we want to do as a family. I want you to see that priorities are developed individually before marriage, but when we come together, we need to communicate our priorities and get on the same page about them. The best way for any couple to manage their money is to agree on their goals and how to get there. Stated another way, the couple agrees on what to prioritize.

Selflessness Personified

This one is for the men. Husbands, if you want to show your wife that you intend to make her needs important, listen to what she wants to prioritize from day one, financially. You will likely be surprised. Some women may want a baller, so they can shop and tear the mall up (don't be so spiritual right now—you know those Jay-Z lyrics)! By and large, this isn't the case. Most women have a far more pressing need than Louboutins. Women want to feel secure. If you can make sure her needs are provided for and some of her wants, when possible, you are going to have a happy wife. Wives require financial security. 1 Timothy 5:8 reads "Anyone who does not provide for their relatives, and especially for their own household, has denied the faith and is worse than an unbeliever." When you begin your marriage, your wife IS your household. Provide for her. Be selfless when we prioritize. She will appreciate you for it.

There is No I in Team

Ladies, I don't want to leave you out of the priority conversation. When you and your mate are working on priorities, always remember the household priorities supersede individual wants and needs. There should also be give and take. No relationship works when one person is getting what they want and the other person is simply providing it and not getting anything they desire. This sounds more like slavery than a relationship. Thirdly, let's be clear there shouldn't be quid pro quo in making financial decision. Give and take in marriage doesn't equal leverage. Satisfying your husband sexually, for example, shouldn't be based on if he brought home the purse you were expecting. Marriage is a team sport. Prioritization is a team concept that we work on for the good of the marriage and reaching our goals and expectations—together. Once we prioritize, how do we make it tangible?

Budgeting

Am I the only person who has "budgeted" my month in my head? I have an idea of what is coming in, I have an idea of what is going out and I make sure all of the bills are paid. This is an example of not knowing where your money is really going and wondering why you don't have any money at the end of the month or the end of the week for that matter. You have to design how to manage your money. Some things may or may not work for some people. Budgeting is not one of those things. It is mandatory. I can't stress it enough. Many of us don't budget. Not because we don't know how, but because we know there isn't enough to pay everything, and we don't want to see it on paper as it will stress us out even more. That excuse is no longer acceptable. When we marry, we join assets and we join debt. We want to work together to manage debt and ultimately become debt-free. Budgeting is how you get ahead with money. Budgeting takes the "crypto" out of "Crypto" Currency. There are no secrets. We know what comes in, we know what goes out. Even when the number is in the red, when you can manage what you have and work to get out of the red, because you can see the deficiency and start to work on how to move forward.

Developing a Budget

Every now and then I ask you can I keep it 100. Not that the entire book isn't 100%, it is, but there are some things I need to be so real with you, I want it embossed in your mind when you close this book. Therefore—can I keep it 100 right here? The quickest way to financial problems is no budget. The quickest way to marital stress is no budget. Burying your head in the sand—no budget. Every business has a budget. Let me rephrase: Every *successful* business has a budget. This is the twenty-first century. You have to manage your finances differently. Interestingly, you might be surprised if you talk to your parents and grandparents and see with those who managed their finances successfully, how many had a budget. Now we understand we need a budget, let's look at how to develop a budget that works for us.

Keep it basic. I'm going to show a very basic budget. You will hear a lot of financial experts discuss zero-based budgeting. Zero-based means you have spent every dollar on paper before the month starts, so theoretically, you have zero at the end of the month. I think this is a great basic budget. What I'm going to share is essentially a zero-based budget. I have attached two pages in the guidebook. Leave the page in the guidebook for future reference. Take a moment and make twenty-four copies of the budget. You have twenty-four months of a very simple budget to start your marriage. Nothing fancy, nothing spectacular, but this is a game plan. Simple game plans are easy to understand and if you do it once a month for twenty-four months, I can promise you at the end of twenty-four months you will be in a significantly better financial position together than you were when you started the marriage.

I spelled out the budget and where to put the numbers. We put a sample page so you can see exactly what the completed budget would look like. This said, I want to explain why it's so important. When you see where every dollar is going, you can manage it. You are in control. It's more of a psychological advantage than physical advantage. A study on Mental Budgeting and Consumer Decisions (*Journal of Consumer Research*, 1996) indicates that mental budgeting pushes us to rationalize purchases. The concept of the budget being inflexible often tempts people to find ways to justify purchases to skirt the budget. This is why we need budgeting. Not as a rule of law, but as our own guide that we design to light our path to financial consistency and freedom.

Tag Team

When we develop a budget as a couple, let me encourage both of you to be involved. I have heard financial experts mention this for several reasons, but my reason is to strengthen your commitment to the relationship. It doesn't matter who makes the most money or who has the best financial acumen, when both people are a part of the conversation, it shows commitment to the relationship. There may be varying degrees of input, for each spouse, but as we learn to budget together, we need to budget...together.

Try to do the budget a little before the month starts. Some people may use a computer or keep the budget on the fridge—whatever works for you. Make sure all of the budget items are completed and it will give you a feeling of awareness and satisfaction with your money you may not have experienced before.

EXERCISE   DATE: _____

MR. & MRS. INC BUDGET

This exercise is for the couples to work on together. I want you to get used to doing a budget together. Let's take fifteen minutes and complete this sample budget with your best estimate. I know you don't have all of your info tonight, but this is practice. Let's just get as close as possible. Put some thought into it. Does your budget look like it can help you save more money? Can your budget help you with tithing? Does your budget make either of your more realistic and comfortable understanding your collective financial situation? Answer these questions to each other.

Zero-Based Budget Worksheet

DATE or MONTH

1. INCOME	BUDGET	ACTUAL
TOTAL		

2. ADJUSTMENTS	BUDGET	ACTUAL
SUBTOTAL		
BUDGET REMAINING		

3. BIG BILLS	BUDGET	ACTUAL
SUBTOTAL		
BUDGET REMAINING		

4. DEBT	BUDGET	ACTUAL
SUBTOTAL		
BUDGET REMAINING		

5. SMALL BILLS	BUDGET	ACTUAL
SUBTOTAL		
BUDGET REMAINING		

6. DAILY LIVING	BUDGET	ACTUAL
SUBTOTAL		
BUDGET REMAINING		

7. SAVINGS	BUDGET	ACTUAL
SUBTOTAL		
FINAL BUDGET (make it zero)		

What's Yours is Mine (Unfortunately)

Your mate is the most incredible person in your eyes. There is no one better suited for you to spend the rest of your life with. When you make that assessment, you also make an agreement. You agree to take on all that is the good, bad, and ugly of your mate. The ugly could be their financial portfolio. Specifically, their debt. Understand that "for better or worse" starts day one. You take on everything they have children, psychological trauma, any other challenges, and their debt. It's now your debt. It's our debt in reality, but mentally, you need to get comfortable with the idea that it is your debt. Why? You didn't create it. Why should you be responsible for it?

When we make the commitment of marriage, we take on the whole of the other person. Also, when any joint venture is moving forward in business or otherwise, the venture must assume all of the assets and liabilities of the organization. Blame is the avoidance of responsibility. Marriage eliminates blame. It doesn't matter who created it, it is now your responsibility.

Talk about your financial situation before marriage. Both parties should go in with their eyes wide open. You should know your mate's financial situation (debt, credit scores, etc.). This is especially true of debt. Debt can be managed if we know it exists and we develop a game plan for it. Get on the same page about what steps you want to take to manage your collective debt.

One important point related to debt is to look at your collective goals vs your financial position. For example, if you want to buy a house that costs $200,000 a year from now, find out what you will need to qualify for the house long before you begin the process of buying the house. Now, take what you learned that you need to qualify for the mortgage and manage your debt in a way to reach that goal. If you know you need to have a 43% debt-to-income ratio to qualify, and you look at your current outgoing bills and add in your new mortgage (subtracting your current rent) and you see that your debt-to-income ratio is 60%, you know you have work to do to increase your cash flow to 43% of your income per month or reduce your debt load. Goals are a great motivator to manage your debt load.

Tithing

I would be remiss if I didn't talk about the importance of tithing to the finances of a Christian couple. I think the mistake a lot of people make is they look at the command of Tithing as a law of the Old Testament. I have heard in discussion that tithing is a law of the Old Testament, it doesn't apply to us today. Let's look into that deeper. As we delve into the topic, let's be honest with how a lot of people look at tithing. Many of us don't have a problem with the theology of tithing, rather, we look at where the money is going and how we feel it is being used. We don't agree with what we see, so we don't give.

Our human intuition sometimes conflicts with our spiritual intuition. We know what God has told us has meaning. We know He provides for us and we know in our spirit that He is good, merciful and truly wants the best for us. Our human intuition is sometimes in direct conflict with our spiritual intuition because it sees with our human eyes. We see megachurches built and church staff being paid, but we may be struggling. This is why Christian marriage is a different kind of love. It's understanding that God's ways are not only higher than ours, but they are different as well.

Tithing is not about what happens with the money once you give. Tithing is about the selfless act of obedience to God and understanding that your financial blessing is tied to your ability to give (not how much money you have to give). God himself says, "Bring the whole tithe into the storehouse, that there may be food in my house. Test me in this," says the Lord Almighty, "and see if I will not throw open the floodgates of heaven and pour out so much blessing that there will not be room enough to store it" (Malachi 3:10). He tells us to bring our tithe (1/10th of our income/increase) to the storehouse. You and your family need to decide the right storehouse to take your tithe to, but the essence of the message is to bring the tithe and allow those who manage it to use it for His work. Your obedience is in the giving, not overseeing the management of the gift.

If our heart condition is good, tithing is less of a challenge. As a couple, learn to be good to each other for the sake of being good to one another. Not because you feel pressured or compelled to do so. The same holds true for the tithe. Share the tithe because you love the Father and you want to give to His kingdom as He continually blesses you and your house. Paul shared in 2 Corinthians 9:6-7, "Remember this: Whoever sows sparingly will also reap sparingly, and whoever sows generously will also reap generously. Each of you should give what you have decided in your heart to give, not reluctantly or under compulsion, for God loves a cheerful giver." Give back to God because you love Him and the condition of your heart leads you to give. Your family will prosper. God loves it. People are blessed through your giving. It's a win-win-win!

Conversation Starter

Sharing stories about how the tithe has blessed someone else or you have been blessed are some of the best stories I have ever heard. It may not be the tithe to the church, per se. It could be an offering to a friend, family member, church member or total stranger. Some of the greatest stories are how giving impacts the life of the giver. Let's take about ten minutes and share a few stories of how giving has impacted our lives and the lives of others.

Chapter Fourteen

Our Business is Not Your Mama's Business

*How to navigate in-laws respectfully, yet keep their
relationship in the proper perspective in your marriage*

One of the toughest things we can deal with in marriage is in-laws. The relationship with the new family is just that—it's new! As the spouse, one of the first things you want to be aware of is that you likely won't measure up to whatever standard every in-law has for you. Different people have different expectations of what Mr. or Mrs. Right is for their family member and you can just about count on the fact that at least one person in your new family won't be your biggest fan. In some ways, it's a good thing. I believe it's good because it's important to understand that the expectations you and your spouse have for each other individually and in the context of your marriage are not going to always be congruent with everyone in your families. The great thing is...that's okay! This is your family. These other people are your extended family. They matter, but they matter as support to your world, not the core. Let's talk a little about why our business is not your Mama's business.

Your Mama Doesn't Get a Vote

If you have seen the movie, "Act Like a Lady, Think Like a Man," you'll remember Terence J's character, Michael Hanover, aka, "The Mama's Boy." His mom (played by Jenifer Lewis) was totally in his business. He didn't live at home, but his room looked like he did. He was totally controlled by his Mom. Jenifer's character was more involved in her grown son's life than any mom should be. You may not run into this extreme, but you may well run into a situation where a mother exerts a significant level of influence in the decision making of her son. There has to be a level of respect between a man and his mother but there has to be a higher level of respect and expectation between a man and his wife. I'm sure you have read it, but it still rings true. Genesis 2:23-24 reads: "The man said, 'This is now bone of my bones and flesh of my flesh; she shall be called 'woman,' for she was taken out of man.' That is why a man leaves his father and mother and is united to his wife, and they become one flesh."

At the beginning of 2:23 it reads 'The man said...' That man was Adam. The first man. He was appointed to name the animals, birds, and livestock. He didn't have a partner and God said it was not good for Adam to be alone, so He put Adam to sleep and made a partner. He brought the partner to Adam. Adam named this partner Woman. Then Adam proclaims: "That is why a man leaves his father and mother and is united to his wife and they become one flesh."

Marinate on this for a moment. Second chapter of Genesis. Barely fifty verses into the Bible. Adam doesn't even have a mother, per se, yet he proclaims from this first marriage that because a woman is flesh of his flesh, when a man takes her as his wife, they are united and become one flesh. What he is really saying is your mom is not a part of this one flesh. She birthed you, changed your bottom, took you to school, bought your clothes and fed you. Put you on the school bus and waited on you every day. Kissed your first boo-boo. This is what a nurturing, loving mother should do. What she also must understand is that when her son gets married, she doesn't have a vote. On anything. Ever. At all. Period. She can make suggestions if requested. She's still a parent, she can offer guidance. Anything more than that, she is overstepping her boundaries. The key here is that husbands have to realize they have to set the boundaries. It is the husband's responsibility to leave his mother and father and unite with his wife. Generations don't develop properly and we don't move forward in our community if men don't learn (decide) to stand on their own feet and make decisions for their lives. This needs to happen earlier rather than later because they need to understand how to manage their own life so they can manage the unity of the marriage.

Personal Declaration of Independence

When you have a taste of independence, the experience is priceless. Independence will require you to make decisions without your mama's permission or influence. Pay bills, decide when to come and when to go. Decide who to date and who to pass on. Independence is going to allow you to face the trials that refine a man for marriage. Independence will teach a future husband how to be resourceful. An intelligent man will quickly learn he can't do everything. As talented, handy, charming, and spiritual as he may be, he doesn't possess each and every superpower. Independence will force you to find out how to get that A/C unit repaired, or how to deal with the fact your cable bill goes up and down like the stock market, but your income doesn't. While you are declaring this independence from mama and daddy, learn this resourcefulness that your wife will appreciate down the road.

I know this book is targeted toward engaged couples, but it's never too late. If you know deep down you could be a bit more resourceful and independent, start taking chances now. It's okay to make mistakes. As a matter of fact, it's necessary! You're not going to be perfect doing this life thing on your own, but you will quickly appreciate that it feels good to make decisions without having to reach out to the consulting firm, Mama, Inc. Mama, Inc doesn't charge much, but with her low costs, she requires a lot of influence and power. You don't need to give up that power in your life at this time. Mama, Inc has your best interest at heart, but what she doesn't realize is that her best interests no longer truly align with your best interests once you accept your future spouse. I would add a bit more to say that you must start to understand that your interests are your interests alone when you leave Mama, Inc.'s building. The benefits were great, but it's time to go find another company to partner with and build a brand. Your declaration of independence has given you the ability to develop a lifelong partnership where you and your partner can still go to your parents for support but ultimately core decisions, insights, thoughts, feelings, and expectations reside with you and your wife.

Oversharing

We have discussed a bit about keeping mom out of her son and daughter-in-law's decision making. Of course, this goes for mom on the daughter's side as well. She can be as loving and caring as she wants to be, but she has to do it from her house and be okay with the decisions you make for your family. This leads me to something that brings on the interfering in decisions and oversharing. Women and men both overshare with family. It's easy to do. We are often best friends with our parents, brothers, and sisters. It's time to start placing boundaries on what we share. Let me explain.

When you have a disagreement or argument with your spouse, when you tell your bestie, she's on your side nine times out of ten. She's got your back, she's there to listen to you and her ear and opinion are necessary. We all need someone to vent with. We need to be able to release frustration from time to time. We don't necessarily need to release all of our frustration to our family. Family always wants their version of the best for their daughter (or son). They often take to heart what you get over in a day. You needed to vent, but they are on the way over to take it up a notch. Family loves you, but this can be a blessing and a curse when you share too much. Not only can they take it too far in the moment, but they often get the wrong impression of the situation and they hold it against the spouse unnecessarily. There are times when a friend or family member may need to get involved (spousal abuse). Short of that, oversharing with family is a bad idea that often has unintended consequences.

The deeper thing about this topic is sometimes you may not even know what happened to create this situation. You could mention some frustration or disagreement in passing to your father. He struggles with the idea someone took his daughter from him in the back of his mind. He uses this information to be aggressive and borderline rude with your husband. This causes friction and either makes your husband want to address it or not come around at all. All of this because of one bit of information that you as the wife mentioned in frustration and have since totally forgotten about. Be sensitive to your spouse and your marriage. If necessary, talk with your spouse about what to share and what not to share. It's not a secret between the two of you. You're not keeping a secret for the sake of the secret; you are protecting your marriage and your relationship with your parents and relatives. Share what you need to with your bestie to talk through a situation. Share what is necessary with your family about your marriage. Don't create an illusion of perfection, that's not healthy either. Sharing is indeed caring but oversharing with family is detrimental.

EXERCISE   DATE: _____

SHARING AN EXAMPLE

Let's get into our groups for about ten minutes and share examples of where your future in-laws or other examples you know of in-law interference. This isn't for the group to get into your business. Feel free to change the names to protect the guilty (or innocent). The idea is to hear examples of in-laws overstepping their boundaries. This is new for a lot of us and we want everyone to see what boundaries look like, what oversharing looks like and what protecting these boundaries look like

Chapter Fifteen

Our Lives Matter!

How to deal with systemic and overt racism

We're in the twenty-first century. The world has changed. The question is how much has it really changed? I don't have to write a diatribe explaining how it's no secret that our children are treated differently on the street, we feel our lives threatened during simple police stops, and our leadership in the country, as of the writing of this book, doesn't condemn overt or systemic racism at any level. The reality is our country has changed, but not all for the better. In general, we don't have to worry about the struggles of the early twentieth century and getting lynched for looking at a woman of another race. That said, we still have incidents like Charlottesville and police brutality on a daily basis, where we do have to learn to protect ourselves, our families, and our marriages from systemic and overt racism. First, let's learn the differences.

Systemic Racism

Systemic racism (also known as Institutional racism) was defined by Sir William Macpherson as "the collective failure of an organization to provide an appropriate and professional service to people because of their color, culture, or ethnic origin. It can be seen or detected in processes, attitudes and behavior which amount to discrimination through unwitting prejudice, ignorance, thoughtlessness, and racist stereotyping that create a disadvantage for minority ethnic people."[4] For the purposes of this text, we are going to use the term systemic racism, because it can apply to any of the world's systems, not necessarily only traditional institutions.

You may be asking "What does systemic racism have to do with marriage?" Everything. Systemic racism can influence where you live, where you work, how much money you make, what kind of person you are attracted to, etc. Every facet of life is influenced by our environment and our environment runs largely on the systems created within it. Check out this example: If you work at a corporation that has a lot of black people in the organization, but you notice that very few get promoted past a certain level and the higher the level you go, the less the opportunity for minorities, then this company, whether they are aware or not, has an environment of systemic racism. We have to understand what this type of oppression looks like to be able to deal with it. I will get into how to deal with it more as we move ahead in the chapter, but as it relates to this specific example, you want to deal with it head on. Have a conversation with management about what it takes to achieve the position you are interested in. Develop relationships, find mentors, sponsors and champions to help you develop the necessary skills to the point that your company and other companies are interested in promoting you.

We often refer to "the glass ceiling" when it comes to gender inequality in the workplace. This essentially means women can make it to a certain point but no farther. We have to work to break all of the obstacles around us and above us. When it comes to race being an issue, find out what the real, unstated requirements for the position are. Sometimes, a company will want a previous salary to be a certain level. They may want a certain level of education. What most companies won't tell you is the right relationships will overcome the system. Before we do a deep dive into how to overcome systemic racism, let's talk about overt racism.

---

[4] Home Office, *The Stephen Lawrence Inquiry: Report of an Inquiry by Sir William Macpherson of Cluny,* Cm 4262-I, February 1999.

Overt racism

When most of us talk about racism, we think of what I'm referring to as overt racism. Being overt is essentially being out in the open, in your face. We can deal with overt racism many ways, but the reality remains that to survive and thrive in our community we need to deal intelligently with overt racism.

When I was about ten years old, someone drove down the street in front of my grandparents' house, saw me throwing a baseball into a net, playing catch and called me the "n" word. I'm guessing most people my age have similar stories of being called a derogatory remark. Much of the time, an individual or a group will do something with a racist overtone trying to push the envelope, to see how far they can go without going to jail or inciting an altercation. We have some people who are more extreme and will get physical or worse. We have to be aware and know how to address this form of racism, to protect our spouses and our families.

Awareness

The first component of dealing with racism (overt or systemic) is to recognize it and be aware of it. Every man, woman, and child of an appropriate age in America, regardless of race or gender should understand racism and the toll it takes on our society. I can't make that happen in this guidebook, but what we can do together is make sure that your family understands what racism looks like and how to deal with it. Overt racism is generally more about the insecurity of a person or group. They are often undereducated and are threatened by certain groups of people because of their own lack of education, knowledge, and wisdom. These people remain a problem, especially when they are authority figures in our society. Regardless of that reality, we have to learn to diffuse situations with overt racism. Non-violence has proven to be the best resolution, time and again, since the years of the Civil Rights movement and that continues to be the case.

Eric Knowles, a psychology professor at NYU, was asked the question "When does racism drive people to commit violence?" His response was, "The most likely predictor of that is exposure to a kind of ideology...But when people come into contact with an organized ideology that valorizes or glorifies an intergroup struggle like a race struggle — that scaffolds from people's everyday prejudices into something altogether more violent."[5]

In essence, Knowles is saying that people must have understanding that the ideology (the system of ideas based on economic and political theory and policy) affects how someone with a racist agenda thinks and behave. Therefore, we know their environment, their group affiliation, their implicit biases, and their inner prejudices determine how people display racism. Being aware of all of these factors helps us understand how to deal with the demon we call racism.

Response

When we consider marriage, we want to make decisions that are healthy for the marriage. I mentioned a person earlier in the workbook who was often frustrated by systemic racism, but he never had any idea how to deal with it. He endured it, his wife endured it, yet he didn't understand how to help his family move beyond it. Once you are aware, you want to develop a strategy on how to move forward, and not be held back by systemic racism or be more fearful of overt racism. How do we protect our families from racism? How do we respond the right way?

 Diffuse situations. I believe it is paramount to make it a point to take down the tone of any confrontation based in race. We must remember, most of the time in any context, it's not about winning or losing a debate. Generally, the point of the conversation is to get the other person or group to understand your side. No yelling, screaming, cursing. No getting on your soap box about how you have been wronged. Chill. Marinate for a moment. Try to understand their mindset, then calm the situation down and be willing to share your perspective to help them understand where you are coming from. When we relate to one another, we get more done.

---

[5] Kaplan, Sarah and William Wan. "Why are People Still Racist? What Science Says about America's Race Problem." The Washington Post, August 14, 2017. https://www.washingtonpost.com/news/speaking-of-science/wp/2017/08/14/why-are-people-still-racist-what-science-says-about-americas-race-problem/

Non-violence. This is the result of diffusing a situation. Escalating any situation dealing with race is not good for anyone involved. Many of us have been in situations where we felt like violence was justified. Being justified won't help you if you don't get home to your family. Non-violence is required in conversations and confrontations dealing with race. We must keep cool heads.

Start a movement or put yourself in a place to influence change. Colin Kaepernick started an important movement by taking a knee during the national anthem at NFL games. Things that initiate movement by a group of people influence change at a macro level, even if it takes time to realize all of the benefits of change. Maybe if you are dealing with systemic racism on your job, starting a movement isn't going to influence change. What is possible in corporate America is racially conscious people (black or white) can ascend to positions where they can enact policies and procedures that influence change. Even more important than the policies and procedures is influencing the climate and culture of the workplace. Changing hearts and minds is far more important and effective than implementing rules—though rules have their place. Influencing the change of mindsets is the most difficult response to racism, but it is the most effective.

Don't do anything. Racism is symbolic of superiority and indicative of insecurity. An example of this is in Brazil. Whites and blacks live in integrated societies, but black Brazilians are thought of as poor and often ignored as though they don't exist in social settings. Think about that for a moment. We deal with people not treating us as we should be treated but imagine being treated as though you are invisible. It's degradation on a higher level. I share this to communicate that the best response sometimes to racism is not to do anything. Asking for someone to see me who doesn't is a waste of my time. Asking for someone to hear me to who doesn't want to hear me is a waste of my time and resources. If someone is barking just to be barking, but they have no relevance, they simply want to get under your skin or "fire up their base," don't take the bait. The best example of this is social media. People find bravado they would never have in person to say things on Facebook and Twitter. Fighting those battles is a waste of time and could wind up being detrimental to you in the long run. Employers often look at social media to see your commentary and they may make hiring decisions based on your social media profile. You can't get a job by talking crazy on Facebook, but you can definitely lose one. Be selective in your fight, some battles aren't worth it. Some battles would never exist if you don't fan the flame of ignorance.

Call out people who make racist remarks in your social circle. It won't be popular and you may think you are stepping out of bounds but you aren't. Remember, this work is about making your marriage better and you want to set the tone for your household. You expect your spouse and your children to stand up for the right thing, whether an aggressor is saying something racist or a friend, family member, co-worker or client, you have to be the example. If you have values you believe in, show the commitment to these values in these uncomfortable moments. You want your family to know that you want people around your family to be people who share the same values. We can't get better and heal as a society if we don't start with the man in the mirror (I don't think Michael's estate can make me pay for that).

Talk to each other, find commonalities and relate. As we mentioned earlier, people develop mindsets through ideologies. Some executives may think black people aren't fit to be in the C-suite because their bosses said something to that extent or created that narrative. Some people don't interact with black people very much. They live in a bubble, so to speak. It is no one's fault, it's just a reality. Their narrative is built off of local news, CNN, Fox News, reality tv and YouTube. They really don't know what they don't know. The more we make a conscious decision to talk to each other, the more we find out how we relate. We have many of the same hardships and challenges. Although this program points out some of the things that differentiate us as a culture, there is a lot we can relate to if we take the time to learn about one another. Building relationships brings people together in ways that firing shots on social media could never accomplish. Speak a little, listen a lot...learn about how people with skewed perspectives developed their mindset. Discuss commonalities. You will be surprised how much influence you may have with one conversation or building one significant relationship.

EXERCISE

DATE:

SHARING AN EXPERIENCE

Share your experiences and thoughts on how to productively deal with racism. This forum is not designed as a book categorically telling you what to do as a couple. This forum was designed for you to work together with your future spouse and others and work out how to have productive and successful marriages in our community. Let's take about fifteen minutes and share some of our experiences with both systemic and overt racism. The point here is not to just bring up how white people or people in other cultures have disrespected you, the goal is to get each other talking about viable solutions to these issues when they occur. A lot of us sit in silence because we don't know how to address systemic racism appropriately in the workplace or otherwise. We don't know how to respond to overt racism sometimes because any response could escalate the situation. Talk about some of the things you have been through and how you dealt with the situation. Again, this isn't about white bashing, this is about helping all of us learn to build a more perfect union, with liberty, equality and justice for all.

Chapter Sixteen

The 6th Love Language

Understanding how body language communicates more than words with our spouse.

Body language is the language you and I are most fluent in and we don't even know it. Body language is clearly a form of communication, but it is so incredibly important in how we deliver and receive it, I decided it needed its own chapter outside of the communication chapter. The title of the chapter reads as such because Body Language is indeed the 6th Love Language. It communicates love, affection, wants, desires and needs often more clearly and directly than our words ever will. Body language says everything when you can't say anything.

Why is Body Language Important?

If you have been on this planet for any substantial length of time and interacted with the opposite sex, you know they can say a thousand words with a sigh, a wink, a slumped shoulder, holding their head in their hands or sticking their chest out with confidence. While words can be politically correct or not give the full picture (or even a deceptive picture), body language is trying to tell you the reality of how someone feels, if you know how to understand it.

The way we communicate with our body is important because it is the best indicator of how we are feeling or what we think regardless of what we are saying. I'm sure some of the men can relate to this scenario: When you started talking to your spouse early in the relationship, were there times when you two were engaged in deep, interested conversation and she was playing with her hair? If that was happening, generally she was telling you she was attracted to you and she was into you. She could be debating you and not agreeing with a word you're saying, but she's giving you signals that she's totally digging you and you're missing it because you don't know what to look for. You want to know how these subtle signs can be queues and communication to be aware of and respond to in the right way. Let's look at other components of how body language is important in marriage.

Body Language 101

If you are already into understanding body language, please stay with me. You could be surprised how many people don't understand the context of body language because they haven't been taught. Much of what we learn comes from our environment. The way people communicate in one part of the country could be totally different from another part of the country. Understanding body language is a subtle approach to understanding your spouse better.

Context Clues

Something you want to be aware of is the context of the body language your mate is sharing. Body language can tell if someone is happy or sad, content or despondent, confident or insecure. In your relationship, it's imperative to understand how your mate communicates these emotions. For example, confidence and comfort is often displayed when we turn our torso toward someone when we are talking. A mate who is not happy with you will often speak to you without turning their belly button towards you. Be aware of this sign, so you can work to find out why your mate is uncomfortable. Look for consistent displays in body language and what the context is when you see the language. Is your mate speaking to you but hiding their hands and being stiff in their arm and head motions? They could be keeping something from you. It may not be pure deceit, but it could be that they are unhappy with you for some reason and don't know how to address it. Learning context in this form of communication is important to your relationship.

Touching

Touching matters in every relationship and especially in marriage. This isn't about sexual touch. This is about learning to recognize and show intimacy to your mate without being sexual. Some of us aren't into touch or have physical touch as a top love language and that's okay. What you want to be aware of are slight touches that show you are engaged. A great example is when two people are communicating and sitting side by side and one will touch the other's arm, generally between the elbow and shoulder. It's something I have always been keenly aware of, but I was enlightened in my research[6] to find out that it is a universal sign that we understand each other and we are in agreement as well.

Learn how your partner likes to be touched. Some people like to hold hands. There are women who may not care to hold hands, but they would appreciate a man to give them a hand up or down stairs or out of a car door. Does your partner like to watch a movie together and cuddle? Would they prefer to sit in separate chairs? Would your mate prefer to sit shoulder to shoulder (not too close but enough to touch)?

Feet are incredible communicators of body language. If you are talking to your mate, watch his or her feet. If their feet are pointing in another direction, their mind is already heading in that direction—they are waiting on you to stop talking so they can head in that direction. Your mate has already checked out of the conversation. It's subtle, but it's a trait we all have. Some of us like to have our feet massaged or even put our feet on our spouse on the sofa or in bed. If your mate enjoys this behavior, I encourage you to get used to it, and be aware of it. If he or she is putting their feet on you and they stop for a while, something

---

[6] Navarro, Joe. *What Every Body is Saying: An Ex-FBI Agent's Guide to Speed-Reading People.* William Morrow Paperbacks, 2008.

has changed. Look for these changes in touch.

Fluency in Your Mate's Language

We briefly touched on this earlier, but fluency in your mate's body language is massively important. Your mate's body language is going to speak volumes whether they are speaking or not. Think of how well you speak English. Most of us speak English so well that we pick up on the nuances of how those close to us speak the language. Some people put accents on different syllables, some people shorten words, others put emphasis in places that won't make sense to everyone. If this is a friend, family member, or someone you're very close to, you can pick up on their dialect, or accent almost, instantly. You are interpreting what they are saying without realizing you are interpreting a derivative of what you actually learned as English. You have to get as good with fluency in your mate's body language as you are with their spoken word.

Pay Attention

When people ask what the number one problem I encounter in relationship coaching is, it's always some version of a lack of communication. Often, this is because couples aren't paying attention to each other. You can imagine if couples aren't paying attention to what each other are saying, it's even more complex when we aren't paying attention to each other's body language. Here's a concept to remember: Don't make a decision to start paying attention to their body language when there is a problem. *Pay attention from day one.* Learn what he or she likes and how they respond. Body language is the ultimate tell.

Have you ever given someone a gift and you ask "Do you like it?" or "Does it fit?" and they respond "Yeah, I love it," but they don't look at you when they say it, they quickly fold it and put it away or they point away from you when they respond? They are telling you they like it as a courtesy, but in actuality they aren't that pleased. That's a pretty easy example. Men, prepare for when you agree to attend an event, but she can't find anything to wear, she can't get her makeup right and she seems exasperated. Watch her body language. She could be expressing that she doesn't want to go to the event at all.

Look for the commonalities in her body language. Does she always hug with both arms? Does she always kiss you the same way when you reunite? Does she raise her eyebrows when excited and lower them when disappointed?

Watch for these things as you establish your fluency in her language. What happens over time is when something is amiss, you'll notice it without her saying a word. People can say things to spare your feelings or deceive you, but body language rarely if ever lies.

Ladies, let's also be aware of how his body language comes across on a daily basis. Is he despondent after a bad day or does he want to talk? Does he smile when he's happy or is his resting face looking crazy sometimes (like me-don't judge) but yet he's quite happy? You also want to be aware of what he is telling you through his mannerisms and expressions. Learn what his normal language looks like. Then it's much easier to tell when something is not the way it should be. Far too often, we find out something is wrong when it blows up into something major. This is because we didn't see the signs in our relationship. One of the best indicators to look for is changes in body language. If you pay attention to changes in normal body language behavior, it will save you from the day of ever saying "I had no idea anything was wrong." Now, you'll be able to have discussions to work on correcting challenges before you ever have to say those words.

EXERCISE

DATE:

BODY LANGUAGE

Let's learn a little about each other's body language. This exercise will help you learn a few things about your mate's physical language. Surprisingly, this exercise often teaches individuals things they didn't know about themselves. Here's the challenge: I want each of you to make three faces or actions with your body. At least one of them needs to include your lower body. The person making the gesture knows what they are trying to convey. It's up to your mate to guess what feeling you are trying to communicate. They get one guess, then you can tell them if they were right or wrong, and if they were wrong, tell them what feeling it was. Then change it up and the other mate will offer the gestures. For example, it could be a feeling of disinterest, sarcasm, being overwhelmed or exasperated. There are thousands of feelings. The idea is to learn some of the body language of your mate. You may be surprised by some of the gestures and responses! Have fun!

Chapter Seventeen

I'm Your Ride or Die

*Understanding the essence of what
commitment means in marriage*

I enjoy the meme that says "I am not a ride or die chick. I have questions. Where are we riding? Why I gotta die?" Funny, but pretty good questions actually. Where *are* we "riding?" Is this commitment for me to die or until death for both of us or just me? Maybe I'm going too far with the meme, but the point should be well taken: There is no marriage without commitment. Nothing. Nada. Zero. Zilch. Are we clear on this? I want to drive the point home. Commitment isn't icing on the cake, it's the cake, yo! As I mentioned previously, my wife said when we decided to get married, "I'm not getting divorced. Whatever we do, whatever we go through, we have to work it out." She's committed. My wife is down to ride so to speak and she's committed until death do us part. Every day isn't a bed of roses. She's a rock star, but she's capable of getting on my nerves and I'm sure I live right on her last nerve...right there...that's me! Hi from your last nerve...it's nice down here! Lol! It's true, I can give her a hard time, but it's all in love. Regardless if I'm having a bit of fun like here, or if it's serious, we're still committed long term to this marriage. It's actually an encouraging and healthy way to look at marriage. Let's look at this.

Removing Unhealthy Options

Realistically, there are some situations out there where divorce is reasonable and possibly the only option. This is the outlier and not the norm. Most marriages with two adults capable of putting in the work, divorce is an excuse. It's an easy way out. It may not feel easy in the moment, but it's much, much easier than putting in the work to make your marriage work. I realize there will be many people who read this who have been divorced. I don't write these words to condemn, quite the opposite. I write this paragraph to enlighten. Think of it this way—we love our own lives. We fight for them passionately. If we had a disease that was threatening our life, we wouldn't give up. Again, quite the opposite. We fight fiercely and desperately for the relationship between our body and soul to survive and ultimately thrive. Losing isn't an option. Consider your marriage the same way. Divorce is death. It's the death of a relationship with the mate to whom you have committed your life. Speak against divorce. Take the word out of your vocabulary when related to your marriage. It's not optional, so why consider it?

When you remove options that are unhealthy, such as divorce, you fight differently. You're not always digging each other, but you know innately that you are on the same team. Commitment shows its truest form when things are tough. Christ was committed the entire time He was on the Earth (and before and after for that matter). That said, He showed His commitment through his words, deeds and most importantly for our lives, His action by accepting the cross. That's when His commitment to you and I showed its most powerful form. The same has to exist in your marriage. Commitment has to show up every day in your thoughts, words, and deeds and you have to double down on your commitment on the days when you really don't want to do it. That's what commitment really looks like.

Air Jordan

Commitment is really like air. Air is a part of everything we do. We don't see it. We sometimes take it for granted. Air is weaved into everything, not just life. An engine needs air to "breathe." Turbo engines need as much clean air as they can get to maximize power. Even the computer I'm typing this paragraph on needs air to keep from overheating. Air is not only a foundational component of life, but it is sprinkled in everything we do.

Commitment to our marriage is like air to our lives. It's all over the relationship. Our commitment shows up when we interact and spend time with each other. Our commitment shows through when we are away from one another and we're tempted by any number of things. Our commitment is right there when one person is in a dire situation and the only person than can comfort them is the spouse they are committed to. Commitment is the highest form or agreement in our marriage. It's our bond. Commitment is making our spouse the ultimate priority. Commitment is to marriage what Michael Jordan is to basketball. Jordan transcends the game. Every great player that comes along is compared to him. He has almost become mythical and foundational to what many believe about basketball. Commitment is just as important to every marriage as Air Jordan has been to the game.

Exclusive Support

When we use the term ride or die, we're using slang to say that we expect our spouse to support us through everything, until death do us part. The interesting component to this concept that we don't think about is that the support we need and expect from each other is exclusive. As you grow in your marriage, you will begin to understand that the person who is most important to you is also the one person who will support you through everything. You will find throughout life that friends will come and go in some cases. Family will be supportive sometimes, and not so supportive at other times. People that you thought really had your back at work or in the community may not have your back when times get challenging. The support you get from your mate when nothing is working, no one seems to care, and it seems like the world is caving in on you is unparalleled. Again, we have to get back to putting our partner and their needs first.

When my wife and I discuss how her career or something specific at her job is going, I have to let her know, I'm on her team and I support her first! I may have something to say that doesn't feel good or even feels like I'm agreeing with the other team. This could indeed be true, because I'm trying to be objective in my thought on how to help her use the tools she has to get what she needs at work. Ultimately, I'm on her team though. First and foremost, without a doubt, we're building a family dynasty together and I'm supportive of her regardless of anyone else's thoughts, criticism, shade, or hating. I'm riding for her. Willing to die for her. I can support many people in many things, but it may not be exclusive depending on the circumstances. My support and love for my wife is exclusive in nature and I will always be there for her.

I encourage your family to consider this mindset. Life is going to throw a lot of curveballs. People are going to come and go, some are going to talk about you that you never thought would do so. Some people are going to steal ideas, take credit for your work, try to make you or your spouse look small. Some people are going to be cunning about how they try to take advantage of you or your relationship. My encouragement is to make a decision that no matter what happens outside of your four walls, you make a decision to honor, respect, commit to, and love each other unconditionally. Show the world you have a united front. Everything won't work out. The great thing is that when things don't work out, you have a support system to work through it together. The adversity will make you stronger. Working through the adversity with your spouse will make you love them and appreciate them even more than you do today. Wherever you end up on the ride and no matter the outcome, your spouse knows they can count on you to go through it together. Just like Bonnie and Clyde or Denzel and Pauletta, we're going to ride this out.

EXERCISE

A GAME OF SPADES

My favorite card game is Spades. Spades requires teamwork, trust, commitment and the skill to know how to play the hand you are dealt. We're going to have some fun with this exercise. Let's have a quick Spades tournament! We're going to work on how committed we are to our partners. Divide the room into equal numbers of tables. You will need 4, 8, or 16 teams to make this work. Have each couple partner up. Give everyone the basic rules of spades, have an assistant help a player that doesn't know how to play. We're playing one hand at each table. You have to bid your hand (very important). The team that makes the most books wins their table. If you bid and get set and the other team hits their bid, they win and your team loses. If both teams get set, play another hand. Let's say both teams bid 5 or 6 and one team gets one over, the team with the one book over advances. It's a tournament, condensing tables until there is one champion. For those who don't play Spades, you'll find it's intense for some and a lot of fun. More importantly, when you get eliminated (or win the tournament), talk to your partner about how you trusted each other's bid. Talk about how you were committed. It doesn't matter if you were right or wrong, or won or lost. What matters is that you see a tangible example of how commitment to a larger goal can create success for the family.

Chapter Eighteen

Conclusion

[Love] always protects, always trusts, always hopes, always perseveres.
– From 1 Corinthians 13:7

I'm sure there are a lot of readers out there who have noticed one important thought has been left out of this book. I expect there are some people who have skimmed ahead at certain points looking for discussion around this topic. It's not there. That's by design. You see, being understanding, selfless, listening, communicating, healing, resolving conflict, taking personal responsibility, believing in covenant, sharing a vision, having good sex, working on our finances together, caring for your in-laws, dealing with PTSD, protecting you, learning your body language, and being committed are all intricate and complex pieces of what manifest as the love you share for your spouse.

This is why there is no chapter explicitly on love. These components are all a part of all-encompassing love. 1 Corinthians 12:26 reads: "If one part suffers, every part suffers with it; if one part is honored, every part rejoices with it." The same holds true in our marriages where love is the foundation. All of these parts we have described in this guidebook are components of the body of your relationship. They each deserve honor. Each should be recognized, cared for and taken very seriously.

Use references like this guidebook, books like "The Five Love Languages," "The Nine Tenets of a Successful Relationship" and others to refer to when something is off a bit in your marriage. I have given you sixteen things to give your attention in this book. There are others as well that you want to make sure you are addressing. I selected these sixteen because I believe they are foundational to making sure you start on the same page and you have the right tools to move forward, especially in those first important five or so years of marriage. That said, make sure when you communicate, you're spending time laughing—it's a beautiful elixir for the soul. Make sure when you are resolving conflict, you are being intimate and vulnerable about how you feel. Spend time together. You can't really get to know the depth of your mate unless you spend valuable time with them. Maybe most importantly, understand that the person you are choosing to marry has values that align with yours. Values, much like the idea of love, are comprised of looking at what your mate values and believes in. You will learn their values going through this guidebook. I would encourage anyone who has different values to do something that takes courage: pause their relationship and assess what their values really are. If you marry someone with different values, you will find their values generally won't change. It's the deal breaker that hides itself unknowingly. If your values don't align, please make sure you understand what that means for your relationship and your future.

I wrote this book with one hope in mind. My prayer is that every couple who reads this book or takes the classes wants a great marriage. My hope is that we have created talking points that make you take a deep look at yourself, your mate and your marriage to find out if you are really a fit for each other. If you see that you are still a fit after you have been through this course and exercises, my prayer is that you are committed and all-in from the wedding day until you are separated by the end of life. I see many couples in the black community that don't have the tools and the background to support a healthy marriage. It's not for lack of trying, it's for a lack of skill and support. We're here to help develop some of those skills. We're also building communities for support. We need your help with the support as well. We'll building online communities in each area where we offer the program. We need you to get involved and support each other as you step into marriages. We'll have your program directors tell you next steps to get involved.

I'm looking forward to being involved and meeting as many of you as possible.

May your lives, marriages, and families be blessed. I pray that you become a blessing to pour into marriages and help people with their marriage challenges. I'm honored that you took this journey with us and I look forward to hearing about all of the incredible, successful marriages and lives that were touched in these classes.

NOTES

DATE:

NOTES

DATE:

NOTES

About the Author

 Jay Hurt is the "coach's coach." As an author, international speaker, mastermind facilitator, and relationship coach, Jay offers a unique and strategic approach to relationship and communication. He is a strong proponent of both professional and personal development, as well as being passionate about creating frameworks and principles for coaches in order to help them become more effective communicators and leaders. Jay's background, values and beliefs have led him to focus on the importance of good communication in both business and personal relationships. This is reflected in his frequent teaching, speaking and writing.

Jay has a special commitment to see African American couples thrive and live out Godly principles in both the context of dating and marriage. A significant aspect of his coaching and counseling is committed to helping couples thrive and to face the challenges that many African American couples face.

He is the chief operating officer of the Academy of Creative Coaching, as well as the author of his previously released book, *The 9 Tenets of a Successful Relationship*. He is a frequent speaker and facilitator of mastermind groups.

Jay has been married to Tawanna for over 6 years. They have two daughters, Kristina and Jalen.

CPSIA information can be obtained
at www.ICGtesting.com
Printed in the USA
BVHW010226280221
601049BV00001B/1

9 781734 126181